MAN
WITHIN

MARY WITHIN

A Jungian Contemplation of Her Titles and Powers

DAVID RICHO

A Crossroad Book
The Crossroad Publishing Company
New York

The Crossroad Publishing Company
481 Eighth Avenue, New York, NY 10001

Printed in the United States of America

Library of Congress Cataloging-in-Publication Data
Richo, David, 1940-
   Mary within : a Jungian contemplation of her titles and powers / David Richo.
      p.   cm.
   Includes bibliographical references (p.   ).
   ISBN 0-8245-1924-8
   1. Litany of Loreto. 2. Mary, Blessed Virgin, Saint – Titles.
3. Jungian psychology – Religious aspects – Catholic Church.   I. Title.
1X2161.5.L58 R53 2001
132.91 – dc21
                                                            2001001653

1   2   3   4   5   6   7   8   9   10   06   05   04   03   02   01

To my brother Joseph,
in honor of all his quiet and reliable affection,
and to our mother,
with all our history in her love
dark and bright, past and present
ever one in the Heart of Mary

Contents

Prologue

Mary advanced in her pilgrimage of faith and at the same time, in a discreet yet direct and effective way, she made present to humanity the mystery of Christ and continues to do so. — POPE JOHN PAUL II

All the love in all the hearts of all of us makes the world an All of love. Mary is the most loved woman on this planet. A powerful and loving mother who is loved and loves us all is not an invention of Catholicism. She has an ancient history in the collective psychic imagination of humankind. Only her names have changed over the centuries while her archetypal reality remains the same.

We have loved, contemplated, and invoked Mary all our lives. We were preserving the most mysterious and precious truth about ourselves: she is what we are meant to become. In fact, all the religious figures of our tradition are personifications of potentials and purposes in us. We now appreciate how our beliefs about God, Christ, Mary, and the saints were held in the safekeeping of faith until we were ready to acknowledge them as about us and in us. Having faith was how we were cherishing the divine life of the psyche. We could have realized this only now as the human potential movement is giving way to the divine potential movement.

The Litany of Loreto (Appendix One) is a stirring summation of the highpoints of Mary's place in the divine plan. In this sense, there are blessings in the sound of its words and graces in the images they summon up in us. They are our sounds and the images of our inner life. The titles speak directly to our hearts and even carry and contain our hearts. They are not only praises of Mary. They form a portrait of our essential Self, our intrinsic nature, the depth of our incarnate life and of our redemptive purpose. Mary is the mother of Jesus, and she is our mother because we are who he is.

The first extant manuscript of the Litany of Loreto dates from 1200. St. Peter Canisius in the sixteenth century heard it recited in Loreto, a small town in Italy where the house of Mary is supposed to have been transported from Israel by angels in 1291. Loreto means laurel grove, which is where the house first appeared on the Italian landscape. Medieval people made pilgrimages there and brought the litany home with them. St. Peter had it printed in 1558 in Dilligen, Germany.

The Litany of Loreto reflects so much of the history of the church. The litany was approved by Pope Sixtus V in 1587. Pius VII added the title "Queen of all saints" on the occasion of his return to Rome from captivity by Napoleon. Leo XIII added "Queen of the most holy rosary," "Queen conceived without original sin," and "Mother of good counsel." Benedict XV, during World War I, added "Queen of peace." Pius XII added "Queen assumed into heaven."

The titles are poetic, imagistic, mystical, and mythic invocations that access the feminine dimension of the higher Self of all of us. They do not originate in or make sense to the linear cognitive mind. Cardinal Nicholas Wiseman said: "A litany is not intended to be logical but to be a hymn that combines affection, admiration, and entreaty."

Most of the titles are symbols from the Hebrew Bible that acknowledge the role of the feminine in the mystery of salvation and of wholeness. The titles of the litany with our responses form a profound spiritual guide to and a mysterious mystical code about that wholeness. This is the first book that interprets the Litany of Loreto in this way.

We may never have fully accessed or explored its wisdom and its nurturing potential. We may not have guessed its possible impact on our lives. Contemplation of the litany may allow that to happen. This takes meditating on the invocations and fervently praying them. They are sources that become resources when we cultivate them as gardeners cultivate flowers. In the pages that follow I try to provide the gardening tools.

"Feminine" in this context is not equated with female, nor is it a term that describes only females. It is an energy in the psyche of all humans and all of nature. Energy is a field of movement and activity that puts power to use. This energy combines formative and transformative qualities. The titles of the Litany of Loreto describe and promise the farther reaches of that energy becoming activated—put to use—in us. These ancient titles of Mary are a summary of the qualities of our essential Self. In fact, every religious truth and image is a metaphor for potentials in us and in the universe that we have never dared to acknowledge or release. The titles in the Litany of Loreto describe a goddess as a divine energy field within us, the feminine dimension of the Self.

All our lives we have noticed that Mary is pictured as a beautiful woman. Her beauty is symbolic of divine wholeness. Perfection is associated with the masculine archetype and completeness with the feminine archetype. In the Hebrew Bible Judith disarmed Holofernes—symbolic of the male ego—with the beauty of her face. An object of devotion is beautiful precisely in order that we be drawn to it, and it thereby grants us serenity and strength.

Beauty can lead to devotion. What we have traditionally felt toward Mary is devotion that is responsive to her images and their kindly beauty. Through them we were learning about her love for us. Devotion is sentimentality when it stops with rituals. It is authentic when it results in *devotedness* to her purpose of bringing more love and joy into the world. It is responsiveness to the meaning she has in our lives as an archetype of our feminine powers. Devotion is ultimately union with and in her, that is, full contact with life, psychic, divine, and natural.

A few years ago I suffered a great loss and was in a state of grief. One night I gazed in prayer at a picture of Mary, and I was strongly struck by the warmth and beauty of the smiling medieval Madonna. I felt what Solomon must have felt: "How beautiful thou art, my love, how beautiful thou art" (Song of Songs 4:1). I could feel a release from my pain in that moment through Mary's companionship. My many such directly felt experiences of Mary as a source of spiritual transformation are the origin of this book. I began writing it as a gift of thanks to Mary, and it became a gift from her to me and now to you. That is always the way with her: she gives back much more than ever she asks.

All my books so far have been written as a psychotherapist and a teacher. This book I write in response to the words: "Son, behold your mother." I write as one who knows first-hand of Mary's unmistakable, comforting, and adamantine love. I can tell that the happiness I feel in my love of Mary will take more than a lifetime to experience fully. I have loved her deeply all my life, and I know without doubt that she loves me. Anyone can join in this because her love waits for all of us. This most touching of revelations is awaiting ears to hear it and hearts to hold it. Such revelations are the premises of this book.

Most of what you are about to read was written with a special and unusual intuition I did not have before I began writing this book. As I wrote, I felt I was receiving a message directly from the heart of Mary. In my writing of these pages she continually instilled new perspectives, opened new vistas, adorned my imagination, and surprised me with a knowledge I know I did not have before. It is what she wanted me to know and I pass it on to you. There will never be a poetry large enough to praise her, and there will barely be time to fulfill her only request, that we love the world as she does. Each of us can only begin now.

Popular piety often preserves the profound wisdom of the psyche. In the pious but archetypally meaningful story of St. Catherine Labouré's vision of Mary, she saw the Madonna wearing rings on every finger. Some emitted rays of light that extended into the world. Some gave no light at all. When St. Catherine asked about this, Mary said: "The rays of light are the graces

I give to those who ask; the rings with no light are holding the graces no one has asked for yet." We have not begun to ask what Mary can give. We have not dared to let ourselves believe in her fully. We have yet to imagine how committed she is to us as mother and advocate. In other words, we have not yet fully acknowledged ourselves and our marvelous destiny. Thomas Merton wrote in a poem: "Where in the world has any voice / Prayed to you, Lady, for the peace that's in your power?"

This book draws from Christian, Judaic, Buddhist, and many other traditions. The word "catholic" means universal. A universal Catholic is one who is open to truths from all sources. Such openness is a virtue that leads to the discovery of corresponding truths immemorially preserved in all traditions and ultimately within ourselves. Our psyche indeed contains all traditions as part of our heritage from collective humanity. The Great Mother meets us there, or rather here in our universality.

Mary can stand up to change in worldviews; she always has. My concern is that many Catholics seem to scuttle their fervent devotion to Mary as they mature in age and in faith. Thomas Merton is an example of a mature Catholic for whom this seemed to happen. From 1940 to 1950 he wrote twenty-five poems to Mary. From 1950 till his death in 1968 he wrote only six. For many of us, Mary does not survive our growing up, and that is unfortunate since she carries an ingredient so essential to our spiritual development. Mary has to survive today in a whole new way and, hopefully, that is the way she appears on these pages.

The new direction in Catholicism deemphasizes devotion to Mary, and this is a loss. A pendulum is swinging too far away from the reality and significance of the feminine in our religious consciousness. Protestantism did this and now Catholicism is doing it too. Is there a way to come back to center, to let go of the superstition and the sentimental piety and yet honor the heart and soul of Mary more fervently? I attempt to show a way to renewed and new devotion grounded in the depth of psychic truth. I am hoping that this enterprise will lead us to a self-discovery as stupendous as that of finding God's heart as our own.

The challenge now is to make our devotion to Mary and our understanding of her more adult. This book offers some paths, through text and prayers, to that maturity: visioning her as an archetypal energy in our own inner life, acknowledging her dark side with all its fertile potential, and freeing ourselves from any disabling sentimentality and literalism in our appreciation of her. The result is a love of Mary that stands up to our own personal evolution. The new vision of her is simultaneously a self-discovery. She is no longer the Madonna at a distance but the mother, virgin, and queen in our deepest interior life and in that of all the universe, a divine mirror of human and natural reality in its most exultant state.

I am thankful that as Catholics we learned to express devotion with true intensity and fervor. It is one of the features of religion that is sometimes lacking in other religious traditions. While I was visiting Rome during the writing of this book, the Pilgrim Madonna came to St. Peter's Basilica. This is a statue of Our Lady of Fatima that travels from country to country as a pilgrim of peace. I joined the thousands of devotees who had come to honor her. As I passed in front of the statue of the Madonna banked with flowers and candles, I remember thinking how small the statue was compared to what I expected. I felt there was something so touching about the smallness. It proclaimed humility in the midst of the grandeur of the basilica. The image looked so utterly serene and yet so powerfully present. I felt Mary's presence in that moment and suddenly in the midst of my intent and prayerful gazing a voice inside spoke. "Imagine, that is what is in each of us, something that beautiful and perfect." It was the very point of this book! In effect, the statue had become, in that moment, a vision of Mary, and I was hearing her speak to me. It was not a voice of my mind's making. It was the immortal feminine in the higher Self revealing itself in mortal words. St. Peter's was such an apt place for that connection to happen.

It is so significant too, that my revelation came as I was walking away from—that is letting go of—the experience. This recalls an archetypal story. In the *Aeneid*, the hero Aeneas is visited by a messenger-huntress in the woods. Only as they are parting does he recognize in her the effulgent splendor of his heavenly mother, Venus.

When I returned home to Santa Barbara, I told my breath-taking story to a mentor and cherished friend, Sidney Lanier, a retired Anglican priest and descendent of poets. He said without hesitation—again I was hearing something not conjured by the mind—that the event I described was a completion of my priestly ordination. He said that I had been ordained a priest in the Logos originally, but now was ordained anew in Sophia right there in St. Peter's Basilica. He added: "The spiritual feminine in you was suddenly mirrored by the spiritual feminine represented in the statue."

I wondered later if perhaps all visions are just such realizations of how the transcendent mirrors our psychic depths. Visions grant certitude that division is illusory. The infinite is in the finite not, above it. Mary does not appear to people to bring heaven to our hearts but to expose the heaven in our hearts. And all that remains for us is to feel an exuberant gratitude.

> *I am the mother of fair love and of respect and of knowl-edge and of holy hope. In me is all grace of the way and of the truth; in me is all hope of life and of virtue.*
> —Ecclesiasticus 24:24

> *Statements made in the Holy Scriptures are also utterances of the soul.* —CARL JUNG

Chapter 1

Who Is Mary?

Hail holy Queen, Mother of mercy, our life...

Mary can be contemplated as the woman described in the Gospels. In this view the importance of Mary is based on her motherhood of Jesus. This is the literal view. Mary can also be viewed as the most recent personification of the great mother goddess, her predecessors being Demeter, Tara, Isis, Astarte, Inanna, Cybele, Kali, and all the other goddesses of light and shadow. In this view Mary is important in her own right and the accent is not on her as a person but as an archetype, a living component of the human psyche. This is the perspective of Mary that we will follow in this book. It is not a new approach. In the eighth century St. Andrew of Crete wrote: "Mary is a statue sculpted by God as an image of a divine archetype." No mature religious consciousness in human history has ever been literal in its understanding of stories or persons in scriptures but rather respects them for the spiritual truths they represent.

The name of the mother of Jesus is Miriam, the daughter, traditionally, of Anne and Joachim. Her name hearkens to an archetypal tradition. In the Hebrew Bible, Miriam is the older sister of Moses. She is a major figure in the movement to feminize Judaism today. Miriam placed Moses in a basket and sailed him down the Nile. In Talmudic tradition, she convinced her father to continue building a family when he was frightened by the Egyptian law ordering the death of male Israelite newborns.

Miriam is looked upon as a prophet since she foretold Moses
as the savior of Israel. Reminiscent of Mary and the Magnificat,
Miriam sang a song of victory with the Israelite women after the
crossing of the Red Sea (Exod. 15:20).

We know hardly anything about Mary's earthly life. The historical Mary, like the historical Jesus, is not clearly accessible
in the New Testament. They are described in idealized ways as
prototypes of the life of faith, exemplars for us. The Mary of the
New Testament and of miracles and apparitions is the Mary of
the Ave Maria, the Blessed Mother, the Blessed Virgin Mary, our
Lady. She is the threefold archetypal goddess energy of young
virgin, loyal mother, and wise queen. Those three dimensions
characterized the great goddess in every tradition throughout
history. The mystic philosopher Pythagoras reflected that the
threefold goddess represented the phases of a woman's life: virgin, mother, wise old woman. The ancient threefold goddess,
like Mary, was simultaneously the mistress of the underworld
(virgin), the earth (mother), and the heavens (queen). The three
dimensions also reflect the phases of the moon: new, waxing,
and dying in preparation for renewal.

The excesses of devotion and of theology over the past two
millennia regarding Mary become completely intelligible once
we apply them to the perennially venerated great goddess and
not to the historical Mary. What may seem like idolatry when applied to the woman from Nazareth is entirely appropriate when
applied to her archetypal *meaning* in the life of faith. In fact, no
one has yet praised her enough. There can be no excesses for the
source of and the guide to the mystery of the divine life in us
and in all of nature.

Our exalted titles and beliefs in these past centuries were living
indicators of an intuition that survived in us and was served in
Catholic tradition particularly. We knew implicitly that we were
venerating Mary as the divine mother, not as a literal physical
woman who gave birth to Jesus. If Jesus is the only Incarnation of God, then the literal, historical Mary is the object of
our devotion. But if the Incarnation of Jesus is an archetypal

metaphor—as opposed to a merely literary metaphor—of our own human destiny to bring divine consciousness into time in our unique lifetime of faith, then the mystical Mary is the one we honor. (Religious metaphors are not literary but confirmatory of a spiritual truth known in intuition but unknown in logic. This is the sense in which I use the word "metaphor" in this book.)

The historical Mary is an incarnation of the feminine aspect of God, as are other women in the Hebrew Bible and among the saints. Mary is preeminent, but they are all by grace what we can be by the same grace, here-and-now articulations of divine feminine powers within our psyche. Thus the archetypal Mary is an intrapsychic reality in us that also reaches out from us so that we can make her love visible.

How does the incarnational process happen? How does our humanity find its divinity? Mary is the model. It happens by the gift of grace, the fullness of grace, *and* by surrender and choice, an unconditional yes to our destiny and a commitment to live it in such a way that all the world can benefit. The Epiphany, at which Mary presents Jesus to the Magi, is the symbolic representation of this. When we show love, wisdom, and healing in the world, we present God to all humankind since that is what God is. The wholly yes is a holy yes.

We do not know anything clearly about the historical Mary, but we intimately know the transhistorical Mary because her reality is in our very souls. The Mary of Nazareth is not irrelevant. She is the physical foundation of the Mary archetype, as there was probably an actual heroic or wonder-working woman in the origins of beliefs in mythic goddesses. Ariadne of the labyrinth and Queen Arete, mother of Nausicaa, in Homer's *Odyssey* are described as mortal females who were honored as representative personifications of the great goddess. It is significant that Ariadne is a virgin and Arete is a queen. They represent two of the three components of the goddess.

At Pentecost, Mary received the Holy Spirit and finally knew the truth about herself. In that moment, the literal Mary and the archetypal Mary became one and the same. At our Pentecost, our spiritual individuation and enlightenment, the same thing happens to us. In fact, Carl Jung says there are three incarnations. The first happens at the Annunciation. The second is at Pentecost. Our personal individuation as the third incarnation, the one we are here on earth to achieve and receive. That happens to us when we place our ego in the service of the spiritual Self. This is what is meant in Jungian thought by individuation. We will see how the Litany of Loreto is a useful and enriching path to this enlightening moment. At Pentecost, the literal, historical Mary found her intrapsychic divinity as a human and as a participant in the divine plan. We find ours in individuation, combining a psychological enterprise we achieve and a spiritual grace we receive.

The issue is not whether the historical Mary is important but how she is important. She is the personal vehicle by which the transpersonal mother enters our era. The historical Mary is not the archetype, but her willingness to say yes to the divine design makes her the fitting instrument of an archetypal purpose. The historical Mary is still to be honored while always remembering that she is a means, not an end. Mary, like God and Christ, are means to make contact with a mystery that cannot be contained—only approximately described—in human metaphors.*

The dogmas of recent times regarding Mary are logical conclusions and now can be plumbed for their archetypal meaning, not their literal meaning. For instance, the dogma of the Immaculate Conception is a logical conclusion from the premise that Mary is the mother of God and cannot be sinful at the same time. Her assumption is the logical outcome of her immaculate conception since, if she is without original sin, she is exempt from the results of that sin: death and corruption. But logic is not the only origin of dogmatic pronouncements; there is a long

---

*In David Richo, *Catholic Means Universal: Integrating Religion and Spirituality* (New York: Crossroad, 2000), I expand this concept in detail.

tradition of belief in these events in Mary's life. That tradition is the perennial and collective wisdom of humankind. It is to be respected as an avenue to the mystery of divine life. Religions that accept only scripture as authoritative lose out on the limitless versatility of the truth and renounce much of the precious heritage of our human wisdom.

Tradition preserves a truth we have only recently allowed ourselves to believe: the mystery of the divine life is about the depth of our life and the outreach of goodness from us. Doctrines are callings to us to live out our own most precious reality. The dogmas are code names for a profound identity and potential. Mystics expressed archetypal truth most often in encoded meanings. (There are three levels of meaning in dreams, for instance, as well as in spiritual books and in consciousness itself: the literal, the symbolic, and the encoded or cabalistic.)

The above perspectives are not strictly in keeping with the magisterial teaching of the church. They are a form of systematic theology, the task of which is to reinterpret traditional teachings in the light of contemporary needs and scientific and psychological advances. Such theologizing is found more and more in depth psychology. It was Carl Jung who said, for instance, that the coronation of Mary as queen of heaven was a way of acknowledging the Godhead as a quaternity, not a trinity. The other two sources of a more expansive view of Mary are the mystics and the pious laity. Mystics have perennially described Mary in divine terms, realizing they were referring to the feminine nature of God. And even a brief visit to Italy shows how the people, even those unlettered in dogmatic theology, see Mary as the equivalent of a goddess. But since God is a metaphor for a mystery that cannot be comprehended, why not have goddess as a twin metaphor? Goddess does not signify simply a female version of the patriarchal God. It is a term with its own meanings, as we shall see.

Theologians are ultimately bound by a set of dogmatic limits. They work in a walled garden. Psychologists, mystics, and the people play in a wide meadow. "Come, my beloved, let us go into the field," sings the bridegroom in the Song of Songs. The archetypal Mary, reflecting our soul, is the bride.

The distinction between de jure and de facto may help us understand some of this. "De jure" means in principle. It refers to how something is configured by theory or law. "De facto" means how it is in reality. De jure, that is, theologically and magisterially, Mary is a human being, endowed by God with privileges, who intercedes for us as a heavenly resource. De facto, Mary grants graces directly and is the feminine divine Source, what was always understood as a goddess.

This is particularly evident not only in Italy but in the Mediterranean, eastern European, and Latin American countries. Mary is a human de jure and a goddess de facto. Church teachings such as that on Mary as co-redemptrix have certainly supported this. Popular piety has maintained it. This is not idolatry, only recognition of the feminine that has ineluctably survived in a church that is radically patriarchal. The word "goddess" may turn us off because it has a hoary, pagan, and new-age ring to it. Actually it is only a metaphor for a mystery that is larger and vaster than any of our human words or images can contain or describe.

Here are the opening words of a prayer in an English Herbal of the twelfth century: "Divine Goddess Mother Nature, who brings forth the sun...." People have always found ways to experience the diversity of their spirituality beyond the limits or uniformity of official religion. The feminine religious tradition continued in the ancient patriarchal world in the mystery cults of Isis and Demeter. In medieval times, this style became associated with witchcraft and was a target of fierce suppression, usually toward women. Today personal spirituality is being revived. An irrepressible courage in humanity keeps forming and finding its own means of grace.

The tenacity with which for millennia of Western history both men and women have, in the figure of the Virgin Mary, clung to the veneration of a compassionate and merciful mother attests to the human hunger for such a reassuring image.... This tenacity only becomes comprehensible in the context of what we now know about the millennia-long tradition of Goddess worship in prehistory. —RIANE EISLER

The Divine and the Natural

We see many references to the unity of our souls and nature in the Litany of Loreto. If God is our deepest reality and that of nature too, then God is the fullest evolutionary potential of us and of nature. Jung says: "When you really look inside yourself, you see the universe and all its stars in infinity." The sutras say that Buddha, after a long and rigorous meditation period, suddenly looked at nature and realized it was always and already fully enlightened. St. Francis saw God in nature.

Mother nature can be a metaphor for the vast and boundless interiors of the psyche. A poem by Wallace Stevens says: "Perhaps the truth depends upon a walk around the lake." Contact with nature is as useful a way of finding truth as logic or intuition. Nature is a *means* of grace: "Lying down in green pastures ... beside still waters ... is *how* he restoreth my soul."

Natural metaphors are healing. Nature works by alternations of growth and change, of solution and dissolution, like our own life and relationship cycles. When we find the phases of a particular relationship hard to handle, we can meditate on the phases of the moon. An irritation may remind us to appreciate the pearl-forming oyster. The tree that survives the fire may help us when our world goes up in flames. Nature is a moving affirmation of the psyche and its ever-renewing oneness. Spirituality is thus the spirit of evolution. A spiritual practice grants us the inner resources to refresh and repair the universe as well as receive its gifts. Christ touching the earth to make a healing spittle is the allegory for this.

Our life force is the same as the life force of nature and of God. This is what Gerard Manley Hopkins described as "the dearest freshness deep down things." In a truly spiritual perspective there are no separations between nature, ourselves, and God. Sri Aurobindo says: "The All in the individual gives itself to the All in the universe and receives its realized universality as a divine recompense." All beings realize themselves in love, which is a centralizing power that preserves us from fragmenting. Love comes with graces that support and foster its expansion. Love is grace. There is a loving intent in the universe that wants to exert itself in our choices and actions. The most beautiful of human challenges is to let that happen. The most powerful of divine promises is that it will happen.

"Personal" is not limited to the rational, intellectual, or deliberative in this multileveled world. Indeed, the higher Self, Absolute Being, is both personal and impersonal, finite and infinite, transcendent and immanent. The divine includes the cosmic, and we humans include the transcendent. Ultimate reality is both temporal and eternal, and so are the world and we. We are finding out that it is not a matter of either...or but of both...and.

What evolves in evolution is consciousness. It can follow that what we humans are conscious of in our psyches, evolution is equivalently conscious of in nature. We humans know evolution *from the inside,* and so does all of nature. Evolution is a progressive movement toward spirituality, a higher consciousness free of the limits and biases of an inflated ego—though not free of the ego itself. That is meant to grow into a healthy partner of the Self. The psychic is the fundamental reality of all being, and all being is returning to it. That return shows the destiny of matter to be spirit. The new consciousness of this in physics and the ecology movement are surely our most recent ways of returning to the mother goddess.

Archetypes and Fulfillments

Although our whole world of religious images consists of anthropomorphic images which could never stand up to rational criticism, we should never forget that they are based on numinous archetypes, i.e., on an emotional foundation which is unassailable by reason. We are dealing with psychic facts which logic can overlook but not eliminate.

— CARL JUNG

Edward Edinger defines archetypes as "ancient preexisting patterns of the psyche." They are innate endowments of human consciousness. They appear as characters we see in stories: hero, villain, wise guide, trickster, mother, father, etc. Each one is a field of consciousness that articulates a feature of the undivided Self. Archetypes are thus ways of connecting with reality.

Each title in the Litany of Loreto is an archetype of the essential Self in its feminine aspect. Our essential Self is our intrinsic nature unconditioned by history and unobstructed by the interferences of ego. It is the archetype of God in us as unconditional love, perennial wisdom, and healing power. These divine qualities are incarnated in our very being: the love is in our hearts; the wisdom is in our minds; and the healing is in our souls. We are not complete as human until we activate—individuate— these gifts. It is the purpose of our spiritual practice and the most thrilling grace we can receive. There is an innate inclination in us to let this happen to us and through us. That innate inclination is what is meant by an archetype. It is to the psyche what an instinct is to the body, an irrepressible direction toward our human/divine fulfillment. For the body that fulfillment is life and health; for the archetypes it is wholeness, both psychological and spiritual.

Archetypes are universal themes—cross-cultural, transhistorical, and transreligious (like Mary herself)—in world consciousness, i.e., in the collective Self. The archetypes appear as characters in stories the world over. Actually, archetypes articulate a variety of energies in our own life story and choices. For instance, the energy to live through pain as a *hero,* to find wisdom like a *guide,* to pursue a dark purpose as a *shadow,* to protect as a *mother* or *father* protects, to act as the *trickster* who trips up the arrogant ego and gives it its comeuppance. The Self is the central archetype, *God*'s divine life in us and in nature. The Self is the same as the Atman in Hinduism, basic goodness in Buddhism, Tao in Taoism, the Beloved in Sufism, and the indwelling of the Holy Spirit in Christianity.

Archetypes are agencies of psychic force that nourish us toward our goal of individuation, the manifestation of our essential wholeness. In fact, we were given a lifetime so that we could let this integration happen. *We are here to display in our life routine the design in our psychic depths.* We are here to be God, and God wants that to happen, i.e., there is an irrepressible instinct in us toward wholeness. Our intrinsic nature is always and already pointed in a divine direction. To embody an archetype is thus to fulfill our nature.

All this means there is real authority in us as in Christ, who "spoke as one having authority." A patriarchal church might attempt to deny the archetypal powers that are in us. A mature faith means trusting our inner inclination toward wholeness as a blessing rather than doubting ourselves and depending on ecclesiastical configurations of who we are and how we are to live. As an example, baptism was not meant to expunge the archetypes from us but to encourage their growth through grace. The shadow, for instance, is not satanic and meant to be excluded but a fertile interior darkness to be creatively and usefully integrated (see Appendix Two).

Human nature is our yearning for the spiritual, and divine nature is love that gives itself—arises—in response to that yearning. Juliana of Norwich, a fourteenth-century mystic, experienced this as a revelation from God who said: "I am the ground of your yearnings." The God speaking to her is the same as who she is at the deepest level of her being and at the same time is what she seeks. The soul Source seeks the God Source.

The essential Self enlists the healthy ego as an aide-de-camp for this purpose. The universal Self—the energy of God in us—is mostly unconscious to us; the ego is our unique conscious mind. We act from a healthy ego when we observe as fair witnesses, assess without fear, and act in accord with what we have observed and assessed so that our goals in life can be achieved. We act from an inflated, neurotic ego when we are obsessed with saving F.A.C.E., i.e., compelled to act with fear, attachment, control, or entitlement to special treatment.

Our healthy ego gives clues to the potentials of the essential Self, e.g., its integrity, dignity, clarity, creativity, and all the other virtues. The healthy ego reflects the Self; the inflated ego obscures it. Our healthy ego enters the service of the collective Self—love, wisdom, and healing—when we put humble love, intuitive wisdom, and healing power into practice. This mirroring of the Self by the ego is called an "ego-Self axis," another term for individuation. Incarnation is the spiritual equivalent of and metaphor for this uniting of our personal ego with the cosmic Self.

We can transcend our ego only when we have a secure and coherent sense of ourselves. Only a strong ego can let go of itself. We do this with perfect blissful surrender once we recognize the exciting alternative: an existential axis with the all-fulfilling essential Self. This is how the dissolution of ego is the end of longing and the beginning of fulfillment. The dissolution feels like death to the frightened arrogant ego; it feels like homecoming to the healthy ego.

The Self is a resident divinity in the psyche. The ego thus is meant to be transubstantiated by its Source. The Source refers to the divine origin of the archetypes: "One single light, infinite and incomprehensible, simple, without parts, timeless, eternal, the Source of life" it is called by St. Simeon. Since the archetypes are intrapsychic facts about *us*, the Source is an inner event that resounds in the external world. Rituals, imagination, and art arise from this same inner Source. Events occur so we can find the Source in ourselves. That happened for Mary at the Annunciation when she discovered divinity within herself. It happens for us in moments like that, moments of awareness of the divine within, no longer at a distance. It is the toppling of the unnecessary Olympus, the restoration of far-off paradise lost.

Jung said: "The archetypes are the organs of God in the psyche." This means we are motivated, directed, and inspired more by archetypal images than by concepts, ideas, or plans. In other words, we are still being created through archetypal propensities and fulfillments. The present tense of the hymn "Veni Creator Spiritus" ("Come, Creator Spirit") tells us the creation is still going on. Its form is evolution of the world and of consciousness, releasing the resources of the Source. In the Gospel, Jesus' friends Martha and Mary are personifications of this balance. Martha brings resources; Mary stays by the Source. Bethany, their home, is a place symbolic of that combining of practical love and contemplative love, the ingredients of spiritual wholeness.

The Energy of Mary

Let there be light is better stated as let *here* be light. The Litany of Loreto comes alive in a new way for connoisseurs of light who have made the transition from the literal to the transpersonally meaningful. We are praising Mary as the prototype of the feminine dimension—or energy field—of the divine. The titles of Mary the prototype are those of the divine life and of our life, one and the same at the Source. Our nature is human in its extensions and in its depth divine.

The mother archetype is the central concern of this book. To say that Mary is the mother of God is to say that she is the feminine energy that brings to birth in us a consciousness of our deepest reality, i.e., divinity. The motherhood of Jesus is an allegory of that stature and destiny in all of us. It is already and always in us but awaits consciousness.

To grow to psychological adulthood we need to separate from our mothers and move out on our own. We have to leave the literal mother, but the mother archetype cannot be abandoned, outgrown, or left. It is intrapsychic. It is in us as a component of our identity as humans. Mary serves as the permanent archetype who can remain intact all through life. This is why she is so crucial in the story of our unfolding destiny and of our very identity.

Devotion to Mary increased after the Council of Ephesus in 431 when she was declared Mother of God. Ephesus was sacred to Diana, and the site of her temple was considered holy ground to the people there. This was because of an association with the feminine divinity on that spot from ancient times, predating Diana, the then most recent personification of the great goddess. A shrine was built to Mary on that exact site. Likewise, on Monte Vergine in Italy there stood a temple to Cybele, mother of the gods. In 1119 a church was built there in honor of Mary. Christians easily transferred their allegiance to the goddess under her new name. This is not superstition, but an acknowledgment of the feminine as an inextricable dimension of the divine. That dimension, or field, indicates the formative and transformative powers in grace and nature.

Early people possessed what we have lost: an infallible consciousness of a generative, sustaining, transfiguring power in the unconscious and in nature. That is the feminine wisdom which directs our journey through life. The great mother is not like earthly mothers concerned only with life here but with a larger life that transcends ego concerns. Contact with Mary feels numinous to us, as Marie-Louise Von Franz says: "Whenever we contact the deeper archetypal reality of the psyche, it permeates us with a feeling of being in touch with the infinite."

The invocations in the Litany of Loreto lead us to feel something mighty and boundless about Mary and our relationship to her. Their rhythm imbues us with a sense of physical security and joy. The titles in the litany are in metaphors and symbols since our intellect can never fully absorb the magnificent heritage we have been granted.

The litany depicts the force that can dismantle our arrogant ego so it can enter the service of the higher Self as the healthy instrument it was meant to be. That transformation is what Mary declares in her words: "Be it done unto me according to your word." She was not being passive. She was speaking for the vast potential in the human ego. Her words are our words. They were written not to quote a historical character but to articulate what our destiny can be: only when the arrogance of ego becomes humility can the divine be born in our humanity. Our infancy narrative is the story of how Christ-egolessness outwits the Herod-ego.

Such humility is recognizing that miracles happen to us but that the credit belongs to grace, the Source that awaits our resources to make itself available to the world. An arrogant ego is one in which human effort seems self-sufficient and rejects the need for grace. To say Mary is full of grace is to say the Self is full of grace, and our ego has to be humble enough to honor that. Incarnation happens in just that axis.

Thus the work we do is not enough; another force comes into play. It is grace, the archetype of the assisting force that picks up where intellect and will leave off. This force is a "Higher Power" than ego. It is God as an essential underlying and ordering unity in the psyche and in the universe. Mary's grace stays in touch with us, upholding us, leading us to our destiny. It is the source and goal of our spirituality and holds out the promise of mystical communion.

Images That Mirror Our Inner Life

Archetypes are energies that are manifest in a cornucopia of ways. Among these are strong emotions, dreams, visions, apparitions, imagination, and images. All of these are psychological, spiritual, and religious since those three are interrelated qualities of a single psychic reality. One reality is identified as human with respect to us, as natural with respect to the world, and divine when referred to as God, the noumenon behind phenomena, the spirit behind appearances.

Mythical symbols and images are spontaneous discoveries of our archetypal imagination. They have remained intact for all time and still contain their original power. Mythic images can serve a transformative function, like the mother archetype itself, by recreating and repairing our fragmented wholeness. We fragment when we lose touch with the three dimensions of our spiritual identity: human, natural, and divine.

Mythic symbols can also carry us safely over the thresholds of life. How ironic that ancient and primitive people partook of the power of symbols and rituals of initiation, but we more sophisticated people do not. Images—as opposed to logical explanations—are feminine. Perhaps the iconoclastic fever of the eighth and ninth centuries, Protestant iconoclasm in the sixteenth century, and rejection of images in fundamentalist religion today are, at root, forms of anti-feminism. The feminine is associated with imagistic impression as the masculine is associated with logical clarity. When God is strictly a male force, we humans are not made in the image of wholeness.

Images may work better than words or thoughts to convey divine-human union. This is expressed by Lucius, the hero of *The Golden Ass,* when he admits his inadequacy in praising Isis if he only uses his intellect: "I shall try the only thing a devotee can do: I shall always keep thy divine image and thy holy divinity locked in my heart and conjure them in my imagination." Notice that the image is of an inner shrine, an interior refuge. Imagination has brought the goddess into—and up from—his psyche in an enduring and nurturant way. Our prayerful use of the invocations in the Litany of Loreto have always been perhaps a coded response to a unification that keeps happening in so many miraculous—and perhaps yet to be discovered—ways.

The encoded meaning of images is the cabalistic, secret, and primeval significance that has been known by sages and passed down through the ages to initiates through spiritual disciplines and rituals. It is beyond words and yet there are some words that have approximated and illustrated it. The central point of this coded knowledge—expressed in metaphor—is the truth that there is no dualism in us or between us. There is distinction but no true opposition between body and soul, human and divine, the inner and the outer. These apparent opposites combine and coalesce in the special moment when all our thoughts give way to a sense of abiding all-transcending oneness.* Here time and eternity meet, and so do the individual and the God life within and around her.

Deeper concepts than the ego could fathom found their way into myth and poetry. There must be a poetic dimension to our psyche because our experiences so easily become the images and the poetry we use to tell about them. We can deepen our human story by finding its thematic and mythic meanings. The Litany of Loreto is a poem that gives access to the feminine dimensions of these meanings. The Litany of the Sacred Heart and of the Holy Name of Jesus are complementary in that they portray the masculine dimensions.

Why are litanies so important compared to other prayers? They have been used universally from ancient times to describe and praise goddesses and gods. The Roman emperors and the Egyptian pharaohs were considered gods and were honored verbally and in writing with litanies. The titles generated images in the minds of the devotees. Such images of the gods and goddesses were at the same time images of their own archetypal life. The titles they used in prayer were descriptions of their own divine potentials, a mirror of the human soul as a higher Self. Thus, the vision of the Sacred Heart to St. Margaret Mary displays the unconditional love in the Self that appears in the midst of contemplation. The vision of the Holy Spirit on Pentecost as tongues of fire displays the emboldening wisdom of the Self that comes to us even in the midst of doubt and fear. Prayer for mature believers is not a dualistic conversation but an interior connection to a unitary life in us that transcends ego. Thomas Merton expressed it this way: "If I penetrate to the depths of my own existence and my own present reality, the indefinable I am that is myself in its deepest roots, then through this deep center I pass into the infinite I am, which is the very Name of the Almighty."

---

*The Einstein-Podolsky-Rosen experiment has shown the universe to be nonlocal since separated elements of it, no matter how distant from one another, remain simultaneously in contact with one another. The combination of opposites seems to be verified in this context since, if two interacting particles are separated so that one is given a downspin, the other will take on an upspin!

The Metaphor and Mystery of God

I am is the name of God, none other than the Self.
— RAMANA MAHARSHI

Our religion has suffered from a gender bias. The one-sidedly male God we were introduced to as the only God was the archetype of the domination model of the patriarchy. In that sense, monotheism is limiting and not expansive enough to contain the infinite variety in divine life. This is why recovering the feminine aspect of God is so crucial. It opens us to the infinite in the universe and to the depths of the psyche, both one reality called God. Mary as divine makes for a truly holy family within a partnership model rather than a subjugation model.

We are persons with male and female qualities but the inner depth of us is the Source of all personality. That is the God within, not a person but the Source of all personhood. God is personal in the sense of aware. God is not a person in the sense of a separate and distinct individual as a human being is. The word "God" does not refer to a being (limited) but to Being within and beyond beings (limitless). As Paul Tillich says: "God is not a person but not less than a person." In that Source is the combination of all opposites at the same time. Yet it is neither male nor female, and in fact it does not have any attributes at all. No attributes means unconditional, immediate, and direct. This fits with Jung's statement: "The real nature of an archetype is not capable of being made conscious [defined]." Plotinus made this same point when he distinguished the God who is the Self from the ground of being, which he called "the One without characteristics." He used a simile to describe the mystical experience of fusion with the One: "the flight of the alone to the Alone." He also said it was like having light flood our vision so that all things are illuminated but all we really see is the light that is illuminating them. In all our inner life and in all the universe we see only the Godhead, the light on, in, and behind appearances.

A mystical revelation is not new information about the divine life but a final and incontrovertible realization that the divine life is *our* life. A truly mystical vision is one that confirms the interior experience as the experience of God. The initiates of Mithras in ancient Rome felt an awareness of the presence of a god that nevertheless remained above them. The mystery of Christianity is more unified, like the neo-Platonist vision of Plotinus. Another example is that of St. Paul, who felt the indwelling presence of Christ operative in him through grace, that is, not as distant connection but as immediate union.

There is an emphasis today on the divine as an inner or deep reality within us and in nature. It is also true that the divine is the goodness in us that continually diffuses itself in the world. Our outreach of love is just as much a presence of God as is our inner life. The divine in stillness becomes the divine in action, all one holiness.

In Buddhism the depth of us and of everything is called *shunyata*, utter emptiness/spaciousness, i.e., empty of ego, of concept, of division, and of form. *Shunyata* literally means a pregnant void, the hollow of a pregnant womb. From that emptiness comes all that is. The Buddhist emptiness is the Source and acknowledges no person behind it.

Both the word "God" and words about God in other religions are metaphors for the mystery of how space can be Source, what the renaissance theologian Nicholas of Cusa calls "a mystery, the center of which is everywhere, the circumference nowhere." D. T. Suzuki, a Zen scholar, says: "Some day an accident will unexpectedly cause in you a sort of mental revolution, and thereby you will realize that the Pure Land of Serene Light is no less than the earth itself, and that Buddha is your own mind." Note the trinity again: humanity, nature, and divinity.

God is an intrapsychic reality in the depths of our humanity and in the depths of nature. Intrapsychic does not mean thought up by the mind. It refers to an accessing of the interior truth of the psyche. Intrapsychic divine reality is what Huston Smith calls "the beyond within." Our human depths are not narrow and personal but vast, transpersonal, and universal. They are not limited like persons but infinite like outer space. These depths are what we mean by God, a transpersonal reality of infinite spaciousness in us and in all the universe. Such a mystery cannot be fully grasped, only approached. This happens not by rational thought but by mystical experience. To know God does not happen by thinking but by being *initiated into a realization of our own nature.* This is why the Litany of Loreto is so helpful in our self-discovery; it is mystical, not logical.

What does it mean to say that God is in the depths of us? A poem looks like words on a page, but deep within it is a living truth. We look like mortal bodies, but deep within us is the divine life. The infinite *is* what we call God. The unconditional ground of conditioned beings is thus a context and not a being. As we saw above, a God with characteristics is conditioned and cannot be this unconditioned ground of being. The ground is intrapsychic and intranatural, that is, it is in the vast space in us and in nature. It is unconditional light, not bound or dimmed by time or space. In fact, everything unconditional is one and the same reality, e.g., love, consciousness, and God.

The mystic St. Catherine of Genoa spoke of the intrapsychic nature of God in this way: "Nor can I say anymore: My God and my All. Everything is mine, for all that is God's seems to be now entirely mine. I am mute and lost in God." In *The Interior Castle* Jesus says something similar to St. Teresa of Avila: "Seek yourself in me." The spiritually conscious scientist Peter Russell says: "Be still and know that I am God is knowing that the *I am* is God."

Buddhist tantric prayer is another useful technology in understanding the intrapsychic nature of God. The practice proceeds through four steps resembling those of mystical prayer in Christianity:

1. *Action:* We adore and supplicate a divine Being usually through an image, e.g., Buddha.

2. *Performance:* We are friends and peers of Buddha: we imitate what we celebrate: "Wisdom is an infinite treasure to

people, and when they use it they become friends of God,"
is how this is echoed in Wisdom 7:14.

3. *Beginning yoga:* We *are* the deity and adore our own inner
   life and then go back to our daily, less spiritually conscious
   routine. Prayer to the Source is prayer to our higher Self
   ultimately.

4. *Highest yoga:* We are the deity and venerate our own inner
   life, and we sustain that superconsciousness, or better, are
   sustained by it without cessation.

Prayer in the depth psychology view is the dialogue within
the ego-Self *axis.* We move from dialogue, twoness, to oneness in
mystical union, in which all divisions are revealed as illusory. We
move toward the Beloved; we are with the Beloved; we are the
Beloved. This is the transition in the yogas mentioned above, and
it mirrors the path in contemplative prayer in Christian tradition.

The stages above apply to our veneration of Mary. All our
young lives we loved her as our mother in heaven. We were
supplicants who asked for her graces. This corresponds to the
action stage, the movement toward her while she was *above us.*
As we matured in faith, we began to see that the mysteries of
her life were models and challenges of what we were meant to
be. Then we went the next step, the performance stage; we felt
her *beside us.* Finally we dared to recognize ourselves in her and
experienced her *within us.* We saw that she is what we are, a
progression corresponding to the Yoga stages and to the stages
of contemplative prayer. We now love her in the core of our
souls, as the core. Before we loved a picture, but now we love the
motherly, virginal, royal reality of our own humanness, which
boasts such a powerful Source within. Mary is indeed the new
Eve because she is the new potential of divinity in humanity.

*In a breakthrough, I find that God and I are both the
same. . . . Love God as he is: a not-God, a not-spirit, a not-
person, a not-image; as sheer, pure, limpid unity, alien from
all duality.*   — MEISTER ECKHART

*Other worlds and gods are neither places nor individuals
but states of being realizable within you.*

—COOMARASWAMY

The Eternal Masculine and Feminine

God is an intrapsychic reality who, when spoken of or experienced as the Source of all, is called God the Father or Mother. God is an intrapsychic reality who, when spoken of or experienced as the Incarnation of the Source as a giver of resources, is called the Son, personified by Jesus Christ. God is an intrapsychic reality who, when spoken of or experienced as the love that unites us, is called the Holy Spirit.

The Holy Spirit is the feminine principle in the Trinity. Theologian Yves Congar said that wherever he looked for the Holy Spirit in traditional theology he found Mary. Actually, Mary is not a substitute for but another personification of the same archetypal energy. The Holy Spirit and Mary are not in competition but provide complementary images of the feminine divine. Mary as mother may be more accessible to our psyches, but both are valid metaphors for a vast spiritual presence both within our inner life and containing it.

The purpose of scripture is not historical or expository but transhistorical and revelatory of that inner life, the divine abode. The symbols in the Litany of Loreto are gathered from scripture. They are indicators of what our spiritual Self looks like in its feminine form. The litany evokes the depths of the feminine in the divine, and this is why we still recite it and feel something as we do so. Prayers and litanies last because they continue to evoke the numinous, the divine design behind displays.

The feminine archetype arouses us to nature and to bodily joy. Both are alive in the invocations of the Litany of Loreto. It does not invite thought but passion. This passion is for soulful contact with the world and God. We are drawn to what we are. Since we are whole, we actually combine and contain all the apparent human opposites, including maleness and femaleness as well as the degrees of difference between them. We are beings of both thought and passion, so our wholeness happens in a context of combination, not of separation. Masculine and feminine do not have to be polarities but spectrums that coalesce.

In prepatriarchal times, the divine nature was thought to be entirely feminine. The goddess protected the people and dispensed power and all that humans needed. In pre-Christian times a king was deposed when he was no longer successful. That was the equivalent of his being deserted by the goddess. Thus the feminine was considered the Source of male power. In patriarchal times, the divine was considered predominantly masculine with authority deriving its power from a male God. The divine right of kings in the Middle Ages reflects this belief.

In Catholicism, the feminine was honored in the life of worship but confined to saints. *Latria* (adoration) was granted only to the masculine God. *Dulia* (veneration) was for the saints, male and female. *Hyperdulia* (supreme veneration) was for Mary. Now we can see through these gender-biased distinctions. We can adore male and female energies in any of the ways they come to be personified. To adore is to honor and invoke the wholeness in the Source and within us.

There is an ambivalence in the male psyche toward the feminine, and it arises continually in the history of the church. The Cathars in medieval times were persecuted severely for reinstating goddess worship. At the same time medieval cathedrals were built on the sites of shrines to ancient goddesses and all dedicated to Mary. She is venerated today, and yet women still cannot have status in the church as priests. The patriarchal depths in us fight equality, and the religious depths in us cherish it. Soon the religious powers will win.

The central mystery of the female is that of endless renewal even after death. At the foot of the cross Mary holds the dead body of Christ. She held him in her womb at the beginning of his life. The womb of mothers and the tomb in mother earth is a single image of how life begins, ends, and is renewed. Like the raven, the mother—Mary and the earth—turns death into life.

Every feature of the divine appears in both human and natural images, another clue to the unity that underlies diversity.

Life after death is symbolic of the ongoing and reliable cycles of human and natural life and of the meaning of life as more than temporal. We are not making a passover to an external eternity but awakening to it here and now. Eternity is not an afterlife but the essence of life that is no longer subject to time: "Attired with stars, we shall forever sit, / Triumphing over death, and chance, and thee, O time," wrote Milton. The goal of human evolution is not to escape from evolution or end it. We bridge time and eternity and do not have to cross the bridge we are. Eternal life is not a follow-up to temporal life. This world and our life can be considered the temporal aspects of eternity.

Our task is to realize the relationship of time to eternity in our own psyches, not by abandoning the body but by acknowledging its beautiful necessity in this incarnate world. Perhaps we have not yet believed in the full implications of the Incarnation since we have limited it to Christ as an individual, and not so much to him as the mystical body of the universe. We were and are always transcendent and eternal as well as embodied and temporary. We do not attain immortality but only discover it. That is a feminine process since it is not based on logic but on intuition and contemplation.

The word *anima* means soul, the point of connection between the ego and the Self. It is the affiliative direction in life and "animates" our capacities to relate. The anima is the heart of meaningfulness. The word *animus* means spirit. It is discriminatory and distinguishes meanings. It represents our psyche's disposition to dominate. We require both these inner energies to relate fully and to express our wholeness personally.

The feminine anima operates on lunar/soul power. The masculine animus works on solar power. Here the accent is on analyzing, distinguishing, distilling, and building will power to make things happen. For the animus all is clear from the beginning. Men go out to see. Women go in to see. This is why the mythologem of the heroic journey is so appealing to males. We have a built-in proclivity toward going to find. Women stay to find. Both directions are in all of us.

When a male does not surrender his inflated ego, he may find himself forcibly toppled and humiliated. When a female does not show effort, she may succumb to depression. One-sidedness leads to a synchronous correction. The psyche is naturally inclined toward wholeness and will not work for us unless we are responsive to its inner claim upon us that we allow all our powers to flourish. The anima and animus are the interior soul mates that grant that opportunity to us.

We all have archetypal longings for what Sufis call "the beloved of our own heart." This soul mate is not a person but the anima of males and the animus of females, the contrasexual side in each of us. The Beloved is our whole Self. This is the partner inside that we meet in contemplative prayer. We may fail to see that our ultimate longing is for the actualization of our own wholeness. The adult, spiritual work is to honor the interior archetypal partnership that wants so fervently to happen within us. This is the spiritual purpose of our life and its recondite meaning.

All of us have the powers of both sexes since we each contain our opposite archetypally as anima or animus. The danger arises when the archetypes are split off and become autonomous. They are then destructive and turn against us since they are not integrated. For instance, when the full archetype of Mary is ignored, idealized, or abridged, her energy turns against us by becoming an immobilizing comfort zone instead of a combination of security and challenge—the full purpose of an archetype in our lives. Mary ceases to impel us to work for justice if she is only the celestial mirror of justice granting solace to us when we have been the targets of injustice. To idealize Mary is to be possessed by the light in her and to fail to see the disturbing force for change and for the ruthless dismantling of ego that she can also be for us.

Mary includes both the archetype of mother and that of the anima, so she is the bridge between the cosmic unconscious and individual life. She is the energy that is formative and transformative. She is the mother of our incarnation as she was of

Christ's. Our transformative destiny is to bring the Source to earth and then to return to the Source. Our goal is our Source. Our transformation is entirely rooted in our formation. We are always and already temporal in our bodies and eternal in our highest Self. The divine becomes conscious through human consciousness. That is what is meant by incarnation and it happens to us when the inner masculine and the feminine are finally and inseparably friends.

Finally, in the chart on the following page, based on Riane Eisler's book *Sacred Pleasure,* we can see at a glance the differences between the dominator and partnership models that have often characterized male and female styles of living. The dominator model focuses on a superior-inferior dualism, a sharply divided submission-dominance style in human relating. In the partnership model the focus is on actualization of one's power for good, not success at being in control. Partnership is about affiliation and interconnectedness, not competition; creation, not destruction; relationship, not hierarchy. It seeks to transform conflict, to dissolve it by nonviolence and compassion instead of violence and retaliation.

Hierarchy is not inherently negative. It is necessary in nature and in society. It is negative when it supplants human freedom. When hierarchy serves people and empowers them, it is useful and life-affirming. Reward and punishment are the province of an authority that controls by fear. When we perpetuate the retaliation model in our personal interactions, we support that paradigm rather than the Christian command to love and to forgive without penalty.

The dominator model in relating to women leads to and is based on misogyny. In our society there is a philosophical reverence toward motherhood but often a hatred of actual women. There are people who love the Madonna but are not kind to the women in their lives. It is up to each of us to examine our conscience and confront these contradictions. They usually have roots in our original relationship to our own mothers and require therapy to resolve.

Component	Dominator Model	Partnership Model
Gender relations	Males ranked higher than females	Males and females of equal rank and feminine qualities are honored
Violence	Violence is institutionalized, e.g., capital punishment, war	Accent on nonviolent resolution of conflict
Social structure	Hierarchical and authoritarian; values killing and exploiting	Egalitarian; values giving birth and nurturing
Sexuality	Coercion, eroticization of dominance, and procreation as main purpose of sex	Accent on bonding with freedom of choice and mutual pleasure
Religion	Dogma over nature, patriarchal authority, retaliatory God and afterlife as reward/ punishment	Divine as unconditional love, moral accent on empathy rather than obedience
Pleasure/ Pain	Pain as sacred, submission as the price of pleasure	Pleasure within a loving bond is sacred as is caring and freedom
Power and Love	Power is for control of others and love justifies abuse	Highest power is to love and share light of consciousness

Riane Eisler also distinguishes between the dominator hierarchy in which authority usurps individual purposes and the actualizing hierarchy model in which authority promotes personal and interpersonal growth.

Chapter 2

In Darkness and in Light

> The moon wanes to grant fullness to things.
> — St. Ambrose

Archetypal energies, including that of divinity, have a light and a dark side. St. Clement of Rome taught that God rules the world with his right hand in the form of Christ and with his left hand in the form of Satan. This is the authentically monotheistic view, one that combines apparent opposites as complementaries rather than maintaining the division of the celestial and the demonic.

The titles of the Litany of Loreto are pearls strung together for wholeness. Each invocation is a single unique articulation of the divine feminine. Yet these are idealized titles that require a shadow element to be whole. The exalted image of Mary emerges from a masculine stereotype of the nurturant feminine; it avoids and cancels the wild, destructive feminine, the dark side.

Recently Mary Magdalene has become an archetype in new age spirituality. She represents the passionate side of the feminine. But such a substitution gives up on Mary as an archetype that can include a shadow and express a more appealing humanity. In the descriptions of the litany titles that follow, we will locate and explore the shadow side (see Appendix Two).

The patriarchy upholds and promotes itself by making nature seem dangerous, something to be overcome. When nature becomes suspect, so do women. In medieval times, devotion to the shadowless Mary was directly proportional to the persecution of witches. These were mostly women who had the gift of being close to the earth and of being knowledgeable about its healing flora. Earth is a sacred feminine presence. Mother/woman, like the earth, cannot be controlled or exploited, and that threatens patriarchal plans. "Witches" and healers were therefore suspect and sometimes executed in medieval times. The human mind will seek out scapegoats to represent the dark side if it is missing from the archetypal images around it. Mary lacked a dark side, and other women paid the price for that patriarchal omission.

The shadow of the divine does not denote evil or malice. Its destructiveness is *the painful dimension of initiation,* a condition of our spiritual existence. It seems evil because it evokes the features of life that are not under the control of ego. It is the nemesis—and liberation—of the arrogant inflated ego. The purpose of the shadow of the divine is to grant hegemony to the higher Self, to depose the fearful ego in favor of love, to free the ignorant ego so it can find wisdom and the ways of healing. This dismantling of ego will feel mortiferous, but it is really a helpful comeuppance. The dark side of the feminine is precisely aimed at impressing the ego into the service of the Self so that it can have the status of an associate.

All the ancient images of the goddess as destructive include the theme of regeneration. The symbol of the vulture is an example. She hovers over death, but she then transforms it into her own living tissue and the food for her young. The dark side of the feminine is in its transformative function, and this necessarily involves a destruction. The conditions of existence in nature include pain, death, storms, and stress as legitimate features of evolution. The destructive conditions of nature are friendly in the unfolding of our evolutionary story. In mature spirituality we do not pray for the conditions of existence to be different but for the grace to say yes to them without protest or blame of God or of humanity.

There are two ways of considering the shadow: the shadow of the human will can be evil; the shadow of natural reality is simply corrective. Arson is an example of a human choice that arises from evil intent. A forest fire by spontaneous combustion is a dark event but also a gift of nature that ultimately helps trees flourish. It is not an evil choice for inflicting pain but a necessary condition for growth. It is the dissolving power within nature that preserves her opportunity to evolve. Corrective evil is dark for light; willed evil is dark for dark.

The historical Mary had a shadow side like all humans. We know nothing about that part of her. The archetypal Mary has a shadow side as all archetypes do. It is not deliberate evil as in the arson example, but natural process as in the forest fire. We invoke Mary against the conditions of existence, and yet the great mother is part of them all. She brings them so she can transform us. We need an appreciation of her that includes this dimension.

Mary is our prompt and perpetual help, and we love the consolations of her presence. Yet we seem unable to meet her as the terrifying mother who helps us grow through pain. Terrifying means frightening to the ego that gives up on the grace behind the terror. To invoke Mary for an exemption from the conditions of existence is to invoke her against herself. Initiatory pain is her dark side. This is precisely how she helps us.

The way of the cross includes both willed evil and necessary evil. The stations of the cross are the necessary dark means to the resurrection. When Mary stays at the cross, she is the sentinel of our spiritual purpose: "to resist not evil" but to stay with it, i.e., bear it, and thereby redeem it and be renewed by it. The image of the women at the foot of the cross is a way of affirming the role of the feminine in the redemptive process. To redeem does not mean to be a victim *of* pain but a victor *through* pain. In this sense, Mary is indeed a co-redemptrix as are we. All this was instinctively known in the spiritual psyche, and so it finds its way into the gospel story. Inspiration of the evangelists means evocation of the inner archetype voice of collective wisdom.

Prayer to the dark side of Mary is thus for strength to bear, not to delete. We would not be respecting ourselves as creatures of light and dark if we wanted Mary to prevent the full journey to happen for us. Instead, we can ask her help in crossing the threshold, not in holding us back from it. That is a way of acknowledging her as a nature divinity having a shadow side. The mother (*mater*) archetype represents the essential goodness of matter either as hurricane or breeze. Looking at the *whole* earth, "God saw that it was very good" (Gen. 1:31).

Other religions have clearer indicators of the shadow side of God. Shiva is specifically acknowledged as the dark element of the Hindu trinity. He is destructive in the best sense since the name "Shiva" means benevolent. His dance in time carries us through the flux of change and crisis. His dark consorts are Shakti and the ogresses Uma, Durga, and Parvati. Destruction and death are part of their and our cycle, not the end of it. The dark side of the mother goddess is not meant to harm us but to awaken us to the givens of evolution, one of which is that things are impermanent precisely so that new life can emerge. The reason letting go makes sense is because we do not possess anything in any permanent way. Our attempt to stabilize what is passing is the cause of so much of our suffering.

If ultimately all is changing, then we certainly have to let go of the belief in changelessness to access the divine reality. We are always being born in some ways and always dying in other ways. The style of nature is to cycle through a sequence of evolutionary transformations, especially in consciousness. This is an eruptive and disturbing process. Mary, Lady of Light and Dark, is the symbol of how consciousness enters history and how we, like Jesus, become God-in-person both on the way of the cross and on the road to Emmaus.

Apuleius writes in *The Golden Ass:* "No one can be initiated unless Isis herself invites him and fixes the day." The trial-fraught journey is a calling and a grace with its own timing. The initiated hero has courage with momentum, the courage to forsake the familiar and move toward a new frontier. This means facing the unknown and making choices with no guarantee about their consequences. A threshold is a crossroads of opposites, at once in and out, familiar and alien, simultaneously cosmos and chaos. Standing there, we are neither out of the old nor into the new. It is the liminal space in which we are nowhere and no one. To be comfortable with such ambiguity requires a feminine energy. At that point, a creative initiative may come. Chaos is, after all, the prime matter—*mater*—of alchemical transformation, the stuff of creation and resurrection: "The people found grace in the desert" (Jer. 31:2).

Even given the importance of timing, Apuleius also addresses this mysterious and touching prayer to Isis:

> O Holy Blessed Lady, constant comfort to humankind, your compassion nourishes us all. You care about those in trouble as a loving mother for her children. You are there when we call, stretching out your hand to push aside anything that might harm us. You even untangle the web of fate in which we may be caught, *even stopping the stars for us if their pattern is in any way harmful.*

Miracles are reversals of nature's laws. The mistress of life's conditions will make exceptions for us at times. This is why our prayer to her can be unlimited in how much we ask. She can bring the dark or avert the dark. Yet our capacity to go on after an ending, no matter how disastrous it is, is the true miracle, not a divine intervention to stop it from happening.

In pre-Christian times the rites of resurrection were celebrated at Eleusis in Greece. Cicero wrote of Eleusis: "We have been given a reason not only to live in joy but to die with better hope." The torch-lit procession there at night was like the one each night at Lourdes. When I visited Eleusis I saw a chapel in honor of Mary on the hill above the ancient pagan shrine. Early Christians believed she was carried there by angels so she too could be initiated in preparation for the Annunciation. The mythical story recounts a touching way of honoring ancient wisdom. Such a legend shows how certain the psyche is that the mother energy is associated with initiation. In fact, after the shrine of Eleusis was closed, people would say as they passed by it: "Forsaken Eleusis celebrates herself." The earth energy of dying and rising is indestructible and outlives the forms of religion and the vagaries of human attention. Mother nature continues the ritual of death and resurrection with or without our participation.

Throughout the centuries we idealized Mary and demonized Eve, thus splitting the female archetype and creating good mother and bad mother images. The task now is to return to Mary her three missing pieces: a shadow, a full humanity, and a connection to nature. Then she can be a complete archetype. This will make all her functions more powerful. She will be the birthing and containing mother who gives us safety and the ego-devouring mother who transforms us. Images of Mary, prayers to her, and theological speculation about her can now include the three missing pieces so that she and we can be whole.

The Great Mother remains true to her essential, eternal, and mysterious darkness, in which she is the center of the mystery of existence. — ERICH NEUMANN

Feminine Graces in Greek Religion

In the *Iliad* and the *Odyssey,* virtuous and courageous acts of heroes are invariably attributed to the kindly and timely aid of a goddess. Grace-giving in ancient Greek religion takes three forms: empowerment for virtue, dissolution of hubris/ego, and inspiration in art and talent. These three activities of the goddess correspond to the qualities we were introduced to in Mary: as mother, virgin, and queen she is the model of virtue. As co-redemptrix she is the initiator of our egos across the threshold of suffering. As mediatrix of graces, she is the dispenser of powers for love, wisdom, and healing. These now somewhat embarrassing titles were not overdrawn; they accurately described attributes immemorially ascribed to goddess energy. I will cite two examples from Greek mythology confirming this. They show the remarkable maturity the collective psyche manifested in ancient religious tradition.

The story of Thetis and Peleus refers to the initiation of the male ego. It shows all three dimensions, or fields, in the feminine

archetype: the shadow, the human, and the natural. This myth presents the dark side of the feminine as a transformative energy. It does this by combining sensuous human relationship issues with contact with the destructive initiatory feminine divinity.

Thetis and Peleus, the parents of Achilles, are shown wrestling on a late sixth-century Athenian plate by the painter Peithonos. The Nereid Thetis was immortal and was humiliated by Zeus's order that she marry a mortal man. She attempted to evade Peleus by metamorphosing into a lion and three serpents. Peleus fought and subdued Thetis. This is the equivalent of dealing with the threshold guardian who becomes an escort into a higher consciousness.

On the plate we see the initiation of Peleus by Thetis before they can be joined in a sacred marriage. We men cannot initiate ourselves. We need a wrestling match with a female archetype for that. In the picture, Thetis stands behind the mortal Peleus embracing him with her divine energy. The lion represents the sun (solar, male power) and the serpents the female moon power. The serpent like the moon sheds its skin and so changes continually. In this way it is an ancient female symbol, since women have moon-cycles. The lion is the same in all seasons and not ruled by cycles. These animal images represent nature's role in the process of enlightenment.

In the picture the serpents of Thetis are biting—that is, opening—Peleus in three places: his "third eye," his ear, and his Achilles tendon. As with all human openings, there is pain in the process. The third eye symbolizes intuitive as opposed to logical wisdom. The spiritual ear is distinguished from the normal ear that hears human sounds. It hears the music of the spheres. The Achilles tendon or heel represents the male ego, his most vulnerable spot. The spiritual feminine is activating the channels of male spirituality. Our cognition requires opening to its spiritual counterpart: intuition and comfortableness with ambiguity. Our ears have to be opened to the music of the spheres, the music it was thought the heavenly bodies emitted as they whirled through the heavens. This is the spiritual music of the larger universe described by Shakespeare as the "harmony in immortal souls." Our arrogant ego has to be opened to the humbling truth that we are not in control or even entitled to be in control. We cannot find these unique and precise initiations by ourselves. They have to be opened for us by a devotion to the archetypal feminine.

Thetis is a water divinity, i.e., spirituality. Water is a female symbol of the death-resurrection. In this instance, the death of the arrogant ego is followed by the awakening to the new life of wholeness. Water dissolves our ego and at the same time, it reflects our image; it mirrors us. Our true self, beyond the limits of ego, is mirrored in the baptismal waters of initiation. The male self has found the fullness of its female, spiritual potential in the goddess and the woman.

Myths abound about female figures who live in water and lure men to their death: Sirens, Lorelei, mermaids. This death is not meant literally. It is the dissolving of the hardened male ego through the waters of rebirth. Isis promises Seti: "I will give you the life-span of the sky." The underlying archetypal theme is that of the female spirituality in the soul blazing a path through death to resurrection. In her reaching out, she drowns our male ego in the waters of death and rebirth. In the home-base she offers, she provides the nurturing waters of spiritual birth.

Contradictories come as no surprise to beings like us whose minds are so nimble at vitiating pleasurable experiences with guilt and rationalizing wrongdoing as right. We continually combine pleasure and pain, good and evil. We hurt those we love. With spiritual practice, our conditional love becomes unconditional. Our narrow habit and bias-bound knowledge becomes wisdom. Our search for someone to fix us becomes self-regenerative and other-regenerative. Such mindfulness cannot be achieved fully by effort, only received in animating grace, as Peleus learned. The story of Thetis and Peleus is an allegory of our destiny for union with the divine in ourselves, in others, and in all of nature.

There is an inveterate fear in the male psyche of women's power. This may account for the archetypes of females with no kindly side, e.g., Medusa, the Sirens, witches. They are to be destroyed or avoided, the only weapons of the frightened ego that cannot imagine integration and alliance. Mary cannot be allowed a dark side as long as men fear women in this profoundly fundamental way. Only when men submit their egos to feminine forces, as Peleus did, are they granted initiatory opportunities. The result is the sacred marriage of the male and female powers within. Fear of the feminine is fear of oneself.

O Muse, sing, in me and tell the story....
— *The Odyssey*

The *nine muses* of ancient myth are personifications of the graces that crown talent with the inspiration to activate it. They were the daughters of Zeus, king of the gods, and Mnemosyne, the goddess of memory. Nine is the sacred number that symbolizes the connection between the divine and the human, i.e., grace. For instance, in the Angelus, a prayer to Mary celebrating her Annunciation—the connection of the human and divine—the bell is rung three times three and then nine times.

The muses are associated with the gratuitous, the grace-dependent, dimension of creativity. Much of the actualization of our potential is not in our hands but beyond the grasp of ego. Each muse is a personification of the feminine power that grants a grace, a tool, for the work we are willing to do. The muses activate and enhance human potential in nine ways. Plato declared the lyric love poet Sappho to be the tenth muse. These are the traditional nine muses with some suggested practices that may facilitate our acknowledging of them as interior energies of creativity.

Euterpe is the muse of music and the emotional responses it brings. She helps us bring harmony to our lives and resonate with the rhythms of the universe. They match our own so synchronously and sonorously. Euterpe also shows us the harmony already and always within us. She shows us how to use our bodies as instruments of this music of the soul and of the spheres, all producing one tune.

Lie or sit comfortably with easy breathing as you listen to music you enjoy. Imagine yourself entering the soul of the music and let it speak to you in words or in feelings. Then draw a picture or write a poem or song of your experience.

Kalliope is the muse of epic poetry and eloquence. Epic poetry is about the bigness of the heroic journey we all make in life. Kalliope in Greek means *voice of beauty*. The full experience of heroism includes a willingness to tell one's story so that others can benefit from it. This means expressing and admitting the dark side of ourselves and our choices.

Tell your story to someone you trust. Write a poem or song about the best and worst experience of your life. How has each of those experiences helped you be the person you are now?

Thalia is the muse of comedy, representing the importance of humor and playfulness in letting the light—and lightness— through. Shelley Glickstein writes: "The hero as fool dives into life's experiences with an unabashed willingness to be humiliated and come up laughing. . . . Until you get the joke, the one you don't think is funny, you are plagued by it. . . . Comedy's happy endings point to reconciliation. . . . It is only inner disarmament that creates the space to receive the greater good that you sense belongs to you. . . . Resilience, the comic hero's elixir, is a function of humility. To be humble is not being lowly but down-to-earth, close to the core, open to that tender force that creates a place for you in the world."

Embarrass yourself by admitting your foibles and your self-centered motivations to any two friends. Find a way to laugh at yourself about something you have been taking very seriously.

Melpomene is the muse of tragedy, who balances Thalia's gifts with a reminder of the inevitability of grief in the journey to awakening. She shows the alchemical value of suffering: its potential for bringing good and compassion out of pain and loss. Suffering enlarges our vision of the conditions of existence so that we see them as *serving* our evolution. Then we collaborate with the inescapable. The Buddha's noble truth is not that all existence is suffering, only that unenlightened existence—that which is still caught in fear and desire—is suffering.

What are you trying to avoid? Experiment with facing it directly and asking what it wants to teach you and what might be its loving intent.

Klio is the muse of history. She helps us contact the arche-typal history of those who have preceded us in our human story. She also assists us in our re-membering of our own past so that we can draw strength and wisdom from it. This is the muse of continuity, kinship with all humans, the value of tradition and of surpassing it, the importance of time, the interior library of ancestral wisdom.

Who are the figures in history that you most respect? What in their lives is something like your own? What is the wisest word they spoke and how can it become an affirmation for you?

Erato is the muse of erotic love. She recommends indul-gence in pleasure. She grants fearlessness in the face of our impulses. Spontaneity and self-trust are crucial to the process of becoming whole. Being swayed by our desires makes them vices—displacements of healthy desire. Healthy desire does not interfere with growth. We were born from desire between our parents. They were representatives of the universe desiring our birth and making room for us. Desire in the course of our lives reveals us to ourselves, gives us initiative, and grants us a sense of competence.

What are the pleasures you forego? What are the excesses you avoid? What would happen if you granted yourself permission to experiment?

Terpsichore is the muse of dance. This is our invitation to *movement* in all directions: ascent and descent, toward and away from center, departing and returning. Every personal choice can become a dance step on the path when we step lively and step lightly. In the course of life we dance alone or with someone or with many people. "Be jubilant my feet...." Dancing as a form of prayer represents evoking a movement in God.

Choose the music you like best and dance to it alone. Then sit or lie and form an image of how you were moving. See yourself opening to wider and more expansive movements with greater skill than you think you have. Now dance again.

Polyhymnia is the muse of sacred song. She arouses the soul to voice its mystical yearnings and to sing about them with joy. She shows how reverence and devotion work together as we progress in spiritual wisdom. This muse makes the human voice sacred. What we say and sing has divine resonance. To sing is to vocalize our call for divine assistance.

Go back to a hymn or carol or prayer from childhood— or to the Litany of Loreto in the present—and ponder the words and tune in your mind or sing it. What does it say to you today about your life and your path?

Urania is the muse of astronomy and metaphysics. She shows us how our own personal identity is written in the stars and how the cosmos lives in each of us. She asks us to know ourselves and the world and God simultaneously as one enduring equation. Heavenly things then are revealed as richly accessible from earthly and inner paths.

In ancient times, the moon was believed to be the threshold between earth to heaven. Souls passed by it at birth and in death. In a sense, Mary's association with the moon is a reference to her role as mediatrix. She offers this to you tonight. Go out into the night for your meditation and sit in silent wonder at the moon and stars. Converse with Mary in her crown of twelve stars and with the moon under her feet.

Restoring Mary

To restore the shadow to Mary's archetype we can begin to picture her as the energy behind the painful givens of existence and as the escort into the purification of ego. This is a warrior energy that expands and complements her image. The pictures of her as the kindly Madonna, the mother of comfort and serenity, represent only one dimension of Mary. As we grow in a more mature consciousness of the variety in the archetypal nature of the divine, we permit more dimensionality in Mary. This is not sacrilegious, only more fully respectful.

To restore Mary's humanity is to see her as a woman and a mother and not as a perpetual virgin in the physical sense. She is not the vestal archetype. Virginity is a phase of her existence. She represents the virgin archetype at first, then the mother archetype, then the powerful queen archetype. This is in keeping with the threefold nature of the goddess throughout the ages.

The three marks of the sacred, according to Huston Smith, fit for the mother archetype: it is not in our control, i.e., beyond ego; it is perennially and incontrovertibly acknowledged as important; and it is beyond our intellectual understanding.

The mother archetype is formative in giving birth to us and transformative in giving us the graces to go out into the world and be reborn. The formative power of Mary nourishes and comforts us as does the "valiant woman" in the Book of Proverbs, an early archetypal image of this dimension of the feminine. We find this in Mary in the images of her in motherly poses and in all we have been taught about her all-embracing motherliness.

Edward Edinger writes: "Suffering—when experienced consciously as part of the archetypal drama of transformation—is redemptive." The transformative power of Mary is in the suffering she models and guides us through, kneading our ego like the true bread that will then rise and be transformed, but only in the dark. This dark side of the feminine archetype has sometimes been depicted as the transformative cauldron—crucible—of witches. Now it can be honored in Mary as the singular vessel within which rebirth occurs. For this we have few images and have received hardly any teachings. This book is meant to open us to such a wider possibility. It is up to us adults in faith to fill out what is missing in Mary's archetype.

In other traditions the female archetype has been unabashedly complete. Apuleius associates Venus, goddess of love, with the dark goddess of the underworld: "Persephone, strike us with the terror of midnight ululations." In India, Kali, a mother goddess, has three qualities: goodness, passion, and darkness. She is motherly and sexual, the human way to be a mother. She is destructive of ego in ruthless ways that turn into the kindest of mercies.

The numinous is fascinating and terrifying. The paradox of the goddess archetype is that it has both fear and love in it. It is the feminine seduction that draws us and the feminine wrath that frightens us. We have been afraid to apply those two to Mary. We have been caught in the patriarchal limitations imposed on Mary. We have not appreciated her ability to hold both shadow and light. Yet she stands comfortably between them as is commemorated in this line in a poem by Cynewulf: "Hail thou glory of this middle world!"

To see Mary's wholeness leads to a discovery of divinity in ourselves that includes the shadow in ourselves. We may fear making Mary complete because it will mean making ourselves complete. It is time to take adult responsibility for our own *disturbing wholeness* rather than to go on dividing the world into angels and demons. Our wholeness is urgently sought by the Source within: "What God wants is for all of you to be holy [whole]" (1 Thess. 4:3). Emma Jung echoes St. Paul: "An inner wholeness presses its still unfulfilled claims upon us." Something in us yearns for completion, a fascinating and terrifying prospect, requiring the aid of a fully developed goddess energy.

To restore nature to Mary is to acknowledge the mother archetype in association with things and places that represent fertility, such as a spring, as at Lourdes, or to vessels such as the Ark of the covenant, or even to helpful animals. Our fascination with miracles is a way of being drawn to numinous goddess energy. The darker transformative side also has a fate dimension. Witch, dragon, grave, sarcophagus, the world of the dead, or anything devouring and inescapable are symbols of this gruesome side. The complete Mary is earth in its heavenward direction. Black Madonnas today may signify this connection with nature. The black is that of the fertile black earth. The dark also represents the mystery of a reality that is still deeply un-conscious. The mother goddess Isis was black too. In alchemy, the symbolic process of transformation of the leaden ego into the golden Self begins with *nigredo,* the blackness. Darkness is so often the connection between living archetypal images that meet, as for example, suffering and resurrection.

So many of the images in the Litany are sensual. Archetypal truths do not stop in the minds but resonate in our bodies. In ad-dition to including the shadow and nature, Mary's image in art and in our hearts is also ready to include human sensuality. Per-haps artists can now bring a respectful sensuousness to pictures of Mary, as we see in images of the Hindu goddesses or in the famous *Madonna* by Edvard Munch. Mary should no longer be the only mother depicted without breasts! Nor does she have to appear as a mother only, as in most pictures of the Holy Family in which she does not look at her spouse, but only at her child. As with images of Christ, she loses her full humanity in the puri-tanical style that depicts the spiritual as if it opposed the material world. This is a denial of the Incarnation as the way divine con-sciousness enters mortal time. Mary is an incarnate energy, not a disembodied spirit. The historical Mary is a connection to this dimension of fleshly sensuousness in the archetype, and it can be pictured, imagined, and taught this way.

St. Bernard in his commentaries on the Song of Songs recom-mends a practice of imaging ourselves kissing Christ's feet as a sign of repentance, kissing his hands as a request for grace, and, yes, kissing his lips as an acknowledgment of union. Mystics, especially St. Teresa, had no problem speaking of their love for the divine in even more earthy, sensuous, or sexual terms. We can still retrieve that mystical daring.

May the Lord only preserve in me a passionate taste for the world.   —PIERRE TEILHARD DE CHARDIN

Chapter 3

Mother, Virgin, and Queen

> *The Tao is the great mother, empty and yet overflow-*
> *ing, bringing for the infinite universe. And it is forever*
> *inside you.* — *Tao Te Ching*

As we saw above, from ancient times a litany has been used exclusively as a list of the titles of divine beings, e.g., gods, pharaohs, emperors. A litany for Mary emerged from the wisdom in the spiritual psyche that knew of the godliness represented in her archetype. Mary is referred to as wisdom present in the moment of creation, as co-redemptrix, as all-powerful. In fact all the titles of God have been ascribed to Mary because the feminine is a dimension of divinity that cannot be denied. A tantric scripture says: "Shiva without Shakti is dead."

We have also seen that the masculine dimension of the divine is found correspondingly in the Litany of the Sacred Heart and of the Holy Name of Jesus. Mary and Jesus are counterpart personifications of the essential Self. Both incarnate divinity in human history and both are what we are. We are meant to become by grace and effort what we indeed are by nature and grace. Jung says: "Whoever speaks in primordial images evokes the beneficent forces [behind them]." Thus to recite the Litany of Loreto is to elicit its graces and empowerments in our lives. It is a spiritual paradox that we can pay homage and be thereby strengthened.

Litany titles are fields of energy in the spiritual world. They describe what is in us potentially and what we are called to display in and disperse into the universe. For instance, the title for Mary "Comfort of the troubled" is a field of energy we are meant to make present in our world. Indeed, we are the way divine comfort is able to reach those who are troubled. This is an implication of the incarnate style of the divine life in time. "I am the Way"—like all the "I am's" in the Bible—is an affirmation of the destiny of the human soul. The mother archetype indicates our inclination to create and nurture, the virgin to serve and contemplate, the queen to exercise authority and protection.

The transpersonal life is present personally in us. We are its real presence when we live out its qualities. When we are mother/ nurturant and corrective, virgin/integral, queen/powerful, etc., we *are* divine feminine love in the world. When we live out the titles in the Litany of the Sacred Heart, we *are* the divine masculine love in the world. Masculine and feminine fields of energy exist in an inseparable unity. Individual consciousness is a unique instance of that unity, just what happens in individuation. Plotinus used the metaphor of a "world soul" that condenses upon earth into numerous individual souls, each a piece of the whole and all of it. As the founder of the Quakers, George Fox, said: "There is that of God in every person."

The threefold form of the goddess as the young maiden, the mother, and the mature ruler are reflected richly in the Litany of Loreto. Mary is honored with specific sets of titles referring to her as virgin, mother, and queen. This replication of the ancient past is not a coincidence but another example of how an inner infallible sense in the psyche of humankind contains one and the same wisdom, no matter in which century or in which religious tradition it appears.

Mary loves us as a virgin by her pure mindful attention to us, as a mother by her nurturing affection for us, and as a queen by her all-embracing protection of us. Devotion to Mary means receiving these three graces thankfully and sharing them generously.

Inciting love in every heart, you bring forth generations.
    —Prayer to Venus, Mother of Rome, by Lucretius (d. 55 B.C.)

Virgin: Resource and Source

Allah has chosen you, Mary.
He has made you pure above all women.
—The Koran

Illusion is a false perception; delusion is a false belief. Separation is an ego illusion. The fall in Eden is precisely the illusion that there is a way to remain separated from our Source. Spiritual awakening is realizing: I am the Beloved within. This is the open space in Zen. It is the ego awakening to itself as nondual, the divine as the deepest reality of the human, God as intrapsychic evolving and ever-renewing energy. A dedication to nondualism is "putting on the mind of Christ," or rather having in ourselves the mind that was and is in him, another way of saying there is no separation. The source of our fear is the separation we imagine between ourselves and God. That illusion continues the Fall into our life experience. A shift in consciousness can set us free and we can realize that what we are is what the divine is. This is what is meant by finding God. Mechthild of Magdeburg, a mystic of the thirteenth century, wrote of "an inward tug by the rippling tide of love which flows secretly from God into the soul and draws it mightily back into its Source." This return of the ego to its Source is simply the abandonment of the illusion of separation.

To say that Mary is a virgin refers to how the archetypal Mary relates directly to the Source. She becomes its resource and delivers the Source to us. The virginity of Mary means that incarnation is about the conception and birth of higher consciousness without the intercession or necessity of any human agency, i.e., ego. The Incarnation is a spiritual reality, not a literal one. The conception of Jesus is special as a spiritual event and ordinary as a physical event. This means that a spiritually virginal consciousness is required if our humanity is to be born into the world of the Self. Christ is the personification of this and is thus, spiritually, the son of a virgin mother.

Beliefs in virgin births were common in ancient times. Many

heroes in the Greek world and even Buddha were believed to
have been born in a virginal way. Only St. Luke tells of the
Annunciation. Only he and St. Matthew mention the virgin conception of Jesus. St. Luke was probably Greek and conscious of
the power of this archetype in god and hero stories. He often
contrasts the kingdom of God to that of the emperor, Augustus.
Jesus offers a new society based on love, nonviolence, and lib-
erty unlike that of Rome. St. Luke may have been attempting to
show the early Christians that Jesus is a new spiritual Augustus.
In this regard, they would have known also of the common belief
that Augustus was born of a virgin. His mother was believed to
have been impregnated by Apollo in the form of a snake while
she slept in the god's temple. Augustus was therefore believed
to be a god. St. Luke says, in effect, here is the real God, born
virginally as Augustus was, but greater and more reliable than
he as the ruler of hearts.

In primitive consciousness, the goddess was parthenogenetic
in the sense that the feminine was sufficient in the origin of life,
its destruction, and its regeneration. Only in the later patriarchal religion was she the wife or daughter of a god or the earth
mother who required a sky father to be a source of fertility. In
the Manichean theology that so many of us inherited, virginity
had an anti-sexual meaning. Mary was above ordinary women
because she never engaged in sex, implying that the choice to be
sexual was somehow wrong or weak. The virginity of Mary is
actually a vestige of a universal theme in the savior story: his
mother is a virgin, i.e., he transcends opposites and overturns
nature's laws.

Virginity in spiritual parlance does not refer to the state of
the hymen. Such literalism trivializes the mystery. Virginity in
the realm of the spiritual psyche refers to the strength and clarity of purpose that opens one to the Spirit/Self so that a new
consciousness can be born. Purity in its loftiest significance does
not refer to chastity or celibacy. To say Mary is pure means that
she is complete. The archetypal Mary is pure and virginal, i.e., in
no need of ego intervention to make contact with or usher in the

Source. The literal Mary is a virgin in the sense of a virgin bride, and bride, like mother, means soon to be sexual. In our Catholic childhood, the almost fanatical emphasis on Mary's purity created a distance between her and us. When "ever-virgin" is taken literally Mary becomes an impossible model. Once the historical Mary is more human, she becomes the archetypal mirror of our own ever-virgin souls.

Virgin means hidden, not yet revealed, like our souls which remain virginal, intact, all our lives no matter how our bodies change. Full of grace is full of gifts, one of which is purity from ego wishes or fears. Mary is the feminine dimension of the psychic powers that are above ego and mere instinct. At the Annunciation she grants life to the Self through the death of ego and the gift of her body. Virginity in this sense is not antiphysical but expresses a spiritual reality. Mary is a spiritual virgin no matter how Christ was physically conceived.

Mary's humility at the Annunciation is a way of saying that the soul of the virgin archetype is tenanted by God alone, not by ego. In her, ego and Self become united. Only in that way could Mary say yes to something that she does not understand. "How can this be?" becomes "Let it happen."

Mary combines surrender and choice in the moment of the Annunciation and that combination of apparent opposites is the occasion of grace. She is full of grace because she is full of yes. This yes was considered passively subservient in our childhood vision of Mary. She was a model of submission in the patriarchal version of her that we inherited. It is time to relinquish that model and see Mary as an active and activating participant in salvation history. That history is our life story once we too combine surrender to the conditions of existence and the choice to love unconditionally. It is not about subservience to alien powers but about entering the service of what is best in us.

Surrender means resonance to the direction the Self seems to be taking in our lives. The things we cannot change, the things that happen beyond our control are that direction, also called the will of God. When control disappears, God appears. Spiritual surrender does not mean giving in. It is not passive or weak. It takes tremendous power and determination to say yes to what is. It is a gift of grace. Our willingness to respond to an unfolding destiny and calling is the essence of sanctity. The archetypal woman we call Mary is the mystery of that willingness, and that is why she is the virgin mother. In Islam, only a virgin can open the gates of enlightenment and guide the soul's mystical passage to a higher life. The virgin-mother symbolism in that tradition fits for the Mary we know too. Mary is an honored figure in the Muslim tradition. She is mentioned in the Koran more often than in the Bible and no other woman is mentioned by name. In the Koran, her birth is presented as miraculous.

The Litany of Loreto addresses the Virgin in a variety of ways. The Advent liturgy says: "O wisdom who came out of the mouth of the Most High, reaching from end to end and ordering all things mightily and sweetly, come and teach us the way of prudence." Mary is called a prudent virgin from the Latin word *providentia,* which means to see ahead.

Mary is called Virgin most venerable and Virgin most renowned from the Latin word *praedicanda:* to be preached. It is up to us to spread the word about who she is beyond literality and how she lives in us as an archetypal energy. In this second millennium we are ready to restore the place of the feminine divine, and Mary is here to give us a start. She is, as we are seeing, an incarnation—like Christ—of the divine life. Mary is the feminine incarnation as Christ was the masculine one. They are prototypes of our destiny.

Mary is called Virgin Most Powerful because it is the power of the feminine in nature and in grace. We have believed the only means for change is effort. To say the virgin is powerful is to say that grace is intact in the essential Self. Human effort is no longer all we have going for us. A resource of grace, full of grace, is in us and wanting to overflow, give birth to a consciousness that is loving, wise, and healing.

Mary is rightly called Virgin most merciful and Mother of mercy. In Hebrew the word mercy in the singular means womb.

In the story of the two prostitutes who found the wisdom of Solomon we read that the real mother was "moved in her womb" (usually translated as "felt compassion," 1 Kings 2:26). The imperative to be merciful as God is merciful is the equivalent of contacting our female powers. The mystic St. Bridget of Sweden heard Mary say: "I am the Queen of Heaven and the mother of mercy. I am the joy of the just, and the door through which sinners are brought to God. There is no sinner on earth so accursed as to be deprived of my mercy." Mother love is unconditional. That is the unique and enduring characteristic of this archetype. It is a call to us to be merciful in that same unconditional way. Mary is the model of this and the assisting force in our finding it in ourselves. Prayer to her and the sense of her energy in us works to foster our compassion.

The shadow appears in the danger that arises from too great an immersion in an archetype. The dark side of the virgin archetype is in the tendency toward scorn for the material world. A commitment to virginity as a consecration to the spiritual may lead to despising of nature and the quotidian life we are here to live. Many saints were caught in a one-sided and body-abnegating lifestyle. This is hiding in a pseudo-ideal to avoid full contact with incarnate reality. Virginity is not an ideal unless it is a choice that makes one more available to the world as a prayerful and compassionate attendant. It is not a refuge from the world because that would be a denial of the Incarnation.

Finally, the virgin archetype may suffer if it is represented as a fear of connection. Since St. Thomas describes spirituality as "a connectedness with all things," fear of connection is a great peril to the soul. Virginity is holy—as anything is—when it means not distance, division, or disdain but respectful and passionate closeness. Nothing about Mary is meant to make her impossible to emulate or to keep her away from us. As long as she is on a pedestal, some of our own most precious life and power is lost to us. In reality, her virginity is the intactness of our own souls and is here within us now.

I am persuaded that the worship of the Madonna has been one of the noblest and most vital graces, and has never been otherwise than productive of true holiness of life and purity of character.   —JOHN RUSKIN

Prayer

Virgin Mary, tug at my soul and bring me to you.

Open my heart to be generous enough to surrender to the givens of my life no matter how difficult.

I am thankful that everything that happens to me is revealing the depth in my soul where you live.

Help me make the choices that lead to a new birth of consciousness in me.

Let it be a consciousness of how much love in is my heart, how much wisdom is in my mind, how much healing is in my soul.

Mary let me be a channel and a resource of this love, wisdom, and healing as you were and are.

Be with me as I give to all those around me the gifts that you give me.

May the openness you create in me become my openness to others.

May the surrender you teach me become my dedication to the needs of the world.

May my choices be pure and universe-directed.

May I be tugged by you all my life till you bring me and all of us to your heart.

Birthing and Rebirthing

The mother of songs, the mother of our whole life, gave birth to us in the beginning. She is the mother of all races and tribes. She is the mother of the thunder, the mother of the rivers, the trees, and all things. She is the mother of songs and dances. She is the only real mother of all of us, the only mother we have. She is the mother of the animals and the mother of the Milky Way. It was she who baptized us, and she has left a memory in all the temples. With her children, the saviors, she left music and dance so we would not forget all this.

— Song of the Kagaba Indians, Colombia

The Madonna and Child are God's supreme truth.
— MICHELANGELO

We have three mothers throughout life: our biological mother, mother nature, and Mary, our spiritual mother. Mother is a metaphor in the case of nature and of Mary. They are mothers in the sense that they represent a structure that acts in a motherly way: forming, transforming, protecting, instructing, directing and redirecting, warning and initiating. This is an energy in the universe called mother nature and an energy in the soul personified as Mary.

The life-giving powers in nature were sacred in ancient times. This referred not only to the physical but to the inner Source that is always alive and one and the same in the world and the psyche. Nature has laws that exert an energy that compels and draws but also accompanies us through the phases of life. Aldobrandesca, a medieval mystic of Siena, when close to death, had a vision of Mary with this message: "Daughters, be obedient to the law of the Mother." The natural and the spiritual mothers are united. Indeed, spiritual and physical growth require a relationship to a mother. That relationship is eternal and crosses all phases of human life from that of a physical mother at birth through a growing appreciation and kinship with mother nature as we mature to the graces of our spiritual mother at rebirth.

Mechthild of Magdeburg saw Mary as the spiritual mother of all humankind: "I suckled the prophets and sages before God was born." Juliana of Norwich saw visions of the motherhood of God and also said, "Our Lady is our mother in whom we are all enclosed . . . and our savior is our mother in whom we are endlessly born. . . . To motherhood belong nature, love, wisdom, and knowledge, and this is God."

Mystics and visionaries spoke in just such archetypal language. They were therefore suspect in the medieval church. More women than men were mystics. In practical terms, they had more time because they were not allowed to have clerical duties. They were thought to be eccentric, but that was because they were such a minority. Today there are so many people opening to the mystical that it feels centered and centering, no longer alien or odd. The Dominicans in medieval times particularly suspected mystical contemplation as a cover for the Protestant rejection of the need for the church and its male-dependent rituals. In a way, this was a legitimate fear from their point of view since in contemplation God is indeed discovered to be present in and as our own interior life! Yet the feminine nonetheless survived in Mary, the only vessel that outlasted the blows of the patriarchy.

Our spiritual destiny is not to become absorbed by an archetype but to integrate it into the intactness of our psyche. We are not meant to be possessed by mother energy but to relate to it. For instance, our own biological mothers are our source and provide a milieu of growth. Our mother is with us at home nurturing and feeding us and giving us a sense of belonging. However, our goal in maturation is not to stay tied to her or be engulfed by her but to grow up as a fellow adult beside her. The dark side of the archetypal mother is an engulfment that can interrupt our emancipation. This containment danger is present especially in the first half of life. In the second half of life, we can return to the mother as a matrix of rebirth. The archetype opens in a new way and the danger becomes a spiritual opportunity.

We cherish the great mother of whom Mary is our traditional personification. Yet describing God as father or mother is functional, not ontological. The words do not define the nature of being but are metaphors for the creative and sustaining dimensions of the divine life, which are the same as the deepest reality of our humanity and that of nature. "The personal history of the experience of the self is the personal history of the experience of God," writes Karl Rahner.

All we have are metaphors for the mystery of that unity. Even the word "God" is a personification since "God is more unlike anything than like anything." We were brought up with a belief in God as the Trinity. Father and Son refer to relationships, not persons. Indeed, the metaphor limps if there is not a mother. The Holy Spirit, as we saw above, is feminine and has mother energy. This is why both Mary and the Holy Spirit appear at the Annunciation. Both are needed to combine the spiritual and the human as elements of incarnation. They are both necessary for the epiphany of a full mother archetype.

We are at the mercy of the dark side of the mother goddess when we do not remain conscious of the shadow potentials in her. She can be destructively controlling, devouring our individuality. She can suffocate us in her embrace, thereby preventing us from developing, making filiation a debt that engenders guilt, and violating our boundaries under the pretext of loving us. These qualities of some mortal mothers are present in the archetypal mother when we concentrate too much on exalting her and having recourse to her without also finding her strength in ourselves. We have had many examples of this in our Catholic past.

The dark side of Mary the mother is thus activated most trenchantly when we fail to acknowledge her archetypal energy in ourselves. The danger is in denying that the power of the mother energy can absorb us. When we see divine maternal power in Mary or in God only, it becomes a force that we are possessed by. When we relate to the mother energy as a reflection of our own souls, we befriend the shadow of the feminine and it becomes our ally. We do this when we acknowledge the dark side of Mary, allow that it is in us too, and choose ever to act in ways that are loving. This is how a befriending integration happens.

A Gaelic hymn of the thirteenth century sings:

O Queen of the saints, of the virgins, of the angels,
O honeycomb of eternal life,
All-surpassing power, presumptuous valor
Goes not far without thee . . .
O Virgin from the southern clime,
May I go to heaven to visit thee.
There is no hound in fleetness or in chase,
Nor wind nor rapid river,
As quick as the mother of Christ to the bed of the dying. . . .

My son Josh, at age twenty-one, traveled to Venice and saw the radiant painting of the Assumption by Titian. He showed me, on the night he returned, a postcard of the painting. I remember him saying as we were both looking at it, "Look how it shows Mary rising up *quickly* into heaven." I thought then, she wants to start helping us as soon as she can. The traffic between heaven and earth from the Incarnation to the Assumption is about this loving zeal of the divine for our humanity.

Rapidity of succor is associated with the divine mother in all cultures. For instance in tantric Buddhism, Tara is the mother of the Buddhas. As the female bodhisattva—the enlightened one who is committed to helping others find enlightenment— she moves rapidly, like a woman immediately responsive to her child's cries. Tara symbolizes the light that makes us Buddhas. She is also Maya, who created *samsara*, the cycle of fear and grasping. Thus she represents a combination of light and shadow. In her red, yellow, and blue raiment she is the goddess in her threatening aspect; in her green and white garb she is the gentle and nurturing mother. Her name means "leads across"— from samsara to nirvana. She redeems and connects the two planes, mortal and immortal. Like Mary, Tara is considered a co-redemptrix. This is not an inappropriate or old-fashioned title for Mary. *The redemption of a race as diverse and complex as the human race requires many redeemers.* Mary is our Christian personification of the female redeeming power.

"I am the queen of all divine powers of hell and heaven," Isis said in *The Golden Ass* by Apuleius. Heaven and hell are interior domains of the psyche. Tara was moved with compassion for the souls in "hell" and released them in an instant. She thus terminates all separations, a power of the feminine divine. The name Tara means "she who hears—or *is*—the cries of those who are suffering and comes to them quickly." She is a personification of the feminine energy in the Self that hears the cries of the ego beset by fear and clinging. Thus the power of compassion for suffering is within us, as is the hell realm of suffering itself. This quality of Tara reminds us of Our Lady of Mount Carmel releasing souls from purgatory. The promise that she would release a devotee from purgatory by the Saturday after his death is another way of commenting on the swiftness of the divine mother to be our helper. These promises and mythologems are not meant to be taken literally lest they become superstitions. They are acknowledgments of the quality of speed and compassion in the intrapsychic feminine archetype of redemption. Thus we notice how at Cana Mary accelerated the entry of Jesus into his public life. There is even a title of Mary as Our Lady of Prompt Succor, the patroness of New Orleans and Louisiana.

Here is an equivalent in a twelfth-century poem to Mary:

> *For thou hast helpen me in may ways*
> *And brought me out of Hell to Paradise.*
> *I thank for it, beloved Ladye,*
> *And I will thank thee for it while I live.*

Buddhist priests in South Korea recently announced what is called a miracle of the flowers in the Chonggyesa Temple in a suburb of Seoul. Flowers related to the ficus plant that appear rarely in Korea are blooming on the forehead of a statue of Kuan Yin, the Asian equivalent of Tara. This blossoming happens when the next Buddha is about to arrive, the Buddha of love, Maitreya. Pilgrims are coming by the thousands to see the white blossoms on the gold statue. Many are now comparing the site to Lourdes because of the healings that are happening. There are twenty-one blossoms mysteriously growing on the five-hundred-year-old statue that is regilded every three years and offers no place for plants to root. The monks say that seeing such flowers is like witnessing the birth of Buddha. The flowers are regarded as of divine origin in India, Japan, and China, and are known to bloom only when a great event for humankind is about to occur. The similarity of this event to Catholic miracles is striking. It is another indicator of the archetypal unity in religious consciousness of the power of the feminine divine.

Prayer

Mother of endless grace, be with me today and every day of my life.

Form me and reform me so I can be born and reborn.

You are here with me and nurture me in ways I cannot fully comprehend or imagine.

You love me and show me how to live with trust in this changing world. You are the changes. You are the stability.

May all that I do and feel today be useful to you in your work for the spiritual evolution of all creation.

May all that I pray for and all my spiritual practice become useful to my brothers and sisters who long to be born and reborn but may not have found the light that leads to your gentle path.

May I be motherly in my love and cherish the motherly love of nature and of you and of my own mother.

I commend to your maternal instincts all those I love and all the universe.

Come quickly to the hell of my desires and fears.

Let me rise with you into the heaven of freedom from ego
and of freedom for compassionate love.

Queen of Heaven

*Now a great sign appeared in heaven: a woman clothed
with the sun with the moon under her feet and on her head
a crown of twelve stars.* —Revelation 12:1

*The crown and halo are symbols of the Self, or wholeness.
... The ego is doing on earth what Christ is doing in heaven
... crowning the Virgin Mary: the principle of material-
ity and egohood is being glorified.... [This is being carried
out] by an ego that is consciously living out the process of
continuing incarnation.* —EDWARD EDINGER

Royalty symbolizes the archetype of the Self. King and queen
are titles that point to the power of the Self to effect change.
Royalty is thus also a symbol of grace. The Kabbalah actually
refers to feminine energy as "queen." An ancient title of the goddess mother was Queen of Heaven. Mary holds and preserves
this title. As mother of all the living, she is the archetype of the
power of the spiritual as it orders and guides the universe. This
is an evolutionary title that acknowledges the role of the feminine in the ongoing work of creation. Evolution in the feminine
dimension is open-ended and ever-newly self-organizing, not an
end already planned out. It is an imaginative process, not a fixed
schema. It is open, not closed, unfolding, not folded.

The Litany of Loreto refers to specific domains of Mary's
queenship. She is queen of the patriarchs Abraham, Isaac, and
Jacob. This title shows the time-transcending nature of the Self
and how it establishes and survives as a continuity through the
generations. The patriarchs lived in the distant past, and yet their
covenants still abide. They continue to guide us by the respect
we show to their memory and traditions. They are our spiritual

ancestors, and Mary is the queen of all of us, the new Eve who rules the world of spiritual promise. She protects and provides our inheritance of evolutionary wisdom.

As queen of prophets Mary enters the present and the future. The prophetic spirit was strongly at work at the Annunciation and Nativity. Zachary, Elizabeth, John in her womb, the shepherds, the magi, and the priest Simeon all acted as prophets foretelling the glory of Christ, that is, the triumph of the spiritual Self over the hubris of ego. Mary is a prophet in her Magnificat. She is first poet of the new order and she is herself foretold by the prophets. Mary is the feminine word that makes flesh the covenant of the ages.

As queen of confessors—or witnesses—she protects and encourages the word that can be spoken by all of us. Cardinal Wiseman wrote: "Mary's place is the very first in the order of Gospel evidences, and so in the economy of faith." She was always regarded as the first witness by reason of the traditional belief that she related the story of Jesus to St. Luke. Mary is the eyewitness of the Incarnation and all that followed in Jesus' infancy and childhood.

Mary is the witness of the three incarnations mentioned above: The first Incarnation happens at the Annunciation and is witnessed by Mary alone. The second incarnation happens at Pentecost when the apostles were gathered around Mary and began to speak so that all could understand the good news of freedom. The third incarnation happens in us when we finally are individuated by letting go of ego and living in accord with the loving design of the Self, the God within. Mary is our witness then too, as the mothering and redeeming feminine.

Mary is queen of martyrs. St. Therese of Lisieux wrote: "If one is completely dedicated to loving, one must expect to be sacrificed unreservedly." Mary oversees the sacrifice of the limited ego to the higher purposes of the Self. The ego does not have to die, only be deconstructed and reanimated in a renewed, reborn condition. This is the painful process of *kenosis,* Jesus' self-emptying at the Incarnation. This is a metaphor for the necessity of self, i.e., ego-emptying for spiritual realization. This was the purpose saints had in mind by asceticism, though they often took it too literally.

Isaiah 53:4 says of the suffering servant messiah: "Surely he took up our infirmities and carried our sorrows, yet we considered him stricken by God, smitten by him, and afflicted." This is a powerful statement of the condition of existence that suffering is part of growth and change. When we are pushed to our limits and we still do not give up, we find out what we are really made of, an irrepressibly redemptive courage.

As queen of virgins, Mary is the archetypal feminine that contains and is the Source. She offers direct access to the Source by showing us it is what we are in our essential being. When our ego is free of fear and grasping we are one with her in purity. Then we acknowledge the Source in ourselves and begin sharing its resources of mercy and joy, as the apostles did on Pentecost. They shared themselves as resources once they were purified of fear. Freedom from fear is contact with the Source.

Mary is queen assumed into heaven. To say she was assumed body and soul is to say that the Self is indestructible by time or age. This is another indicator that the Mary of mystery is not the literal woman of New Testament times but a vast archetypal presence in the world and in our psyche. When the assumption of Mary into heaven was defined by Pope Pius XII in 1950, Jung wrote: "This is the most important religious event since the reformation.... The new dogma expresses a new hope for the fulfillment of that yearning for peace that stirs deep down in the soul, and for a resolution of the threatening tension between the opposites." The assumption celebrates Mary's humanity and how she embodies the divine life of grace. The assumption is a way of saying that soul is an embodied spirit and indestructible by time. Mary's assumption is a prototype of our destiny as humans: to combine grace and bodiliness. It is another celebration of the three incarnations.

The Immaculate Conception tells us when Mary became the special candidate of the archetype: from the very beginning this woman was meant to contain the pure Source without dependency on ego intervention, that is, by grace. Mary is human as historical person and divine as the embodiment of the feminine archetype. The Immaculate Conception is a way of saying that Mary is free of the corruption of the inflated ego represented by the choice of Eve. The archetypal Mary reconfigures the conditions of existence that were thought of as the results of that sin. Now the painful givens of life are not penalties but difficult blessings, since they are the challenges on our heroic journey and we are assured of graces sufficient for dealing with them.

It is useful to pay attention to another dimension in the Eden archetype. Riane Eisler in *The Chalice and the Blade* points out that Genesis was written by elitist priestly males, and thus "it is not Cain's killing of his own brother, Abel, that condemns humanity to live forever in sorrow; it is, rather, Eve's unauthorized or independent taste of what is evil or good." Our theological tradition shows its patriarchal bias when it configures the original sin to be a woman's disobedience, based on curiosity, rather than a man's sin of fratricide, based on hate.

In the archetypal perspective, original sin refers to the innate nature of the shadow, a darkness in us that we inherited and did not cause. It is comprised mainly of three self-deceptions. It is an innate belief in entitlement to an exemption from the conditions of existence. It is an innate inclination to be driven or stopped by fear or greed. It is an innate will to punish and retaliate when we are hurt and to run or betray when we are loved. Original sin is a way of referring to the inflated ego that rejects an axis with the spiritual Self. Thus the phrase "conceived without original sin" is yet another indication that the Mary we honor is an archetype, that is, a personification of the Self, free of ego deceptions. Immaculate Conception is indeed immunity from deception.

The title "Queen of the rosary" was added to the Litany of Loreto in 1614 by the Dominicans. It became official under Pope Leo XIII in 1883. The rosary is not a superstitious ritual. It emanates from an ancient religious consciousness. The rosary is referred to in the *Bhagavad Gita* 7:7. The string is the At-man, or higher Self, that holds all things together. The prayer on each bead corresponds to breaths. This Hindu rosary is sacred to Sarasvati, goddess of language. Hence it has 50 beads for the 50 letters of the Sanskrit alphabet. The goddess hears the words of the prayers and is the Word. The Buddhist rosary has 108 beads. This is 12 times 9 to represent the cycles of the universe. The Muslim rosary has 33 beads for the 99 names of God. In all instances, the rosary is a prayer wheel and a living mandala, a symbol of wholeness.

Blessed Alan de la Roche, a Dominican of the fifteenth century, introduced the rosary to Catholics. In 1479 Pope Sixtus IV commended it as a devotion. It was called "The Psalter of the Poor" because the 150 Hail Marys represented the 150 psalms. In 1557, Pope Pius V, a Dominican, recommended it as the prayer for a Christian victory at Lepanto, and it worked. The victory was won on October 7, and that became the feast of the rosary.

"Queen of peace" is the title appended by Pope Benedict XV in World War I. "Blessed are the peacemakers" is a reference to the feminine pacific quality of the Self so unlike the bellicose ego that thrives on discord and competition. The style of the feminine is the foundation for peace-making: a primacy granted to unconditional love, wisdom, and healing power. This is the opposite of military, retaliatory, and warlike styles of behavior. Peace is the harmony of masculine and feminine, a warrior spirit for justice and a heroic soul for mercy.

May 31 is the feast of the Queenship of Mary. Here is a striking passage from the Third Nocturn of Matins of that feast written by St. Bonaventure, which states some of the themes of this book:

Mary the Queen outshines all others in glory, as the Prophet clearly shows in the Psalm which particularly concerns Christ and the Virgin Mary: It first says of Christ, "Thy throne, O God, stands forever and ever," and shortly thereafter of the Virgin, "The queen takes her place at Thy right hand," that is, in the position of highest blessedness, *for it refers to the glory of soul.* The Psalm continues, "In garments of gold," by which is meant the clothing of glorious immortality which was proper to the Virgin in her Assumption.... She is enthroned next to her Son. Mary the Queen is also the distributor of grace. This is indicated in the book of Esther in the passage, "The little spring which grew into a river and was turned into a light and into the sun." The Virgin Mary, under the type of Esther, is compared to the out-pouring of a spring and of light, because of the diffusion of graces for two uses, that is, for action and for contemplation. For the grace of God, which is a healing for the human race, descends to us through her as if through an aqueduct.... The Virgin Mary is a most excellent Queen towards her people: she obtains forgiveness, overcomes strife, distributes grace; and thereby she leads them to glory.

The dark side of the queen archetype is in her power to show us the path so unerringly that we might not seek it for ourselves. When the church becomes the repository of all truth and theologians are silenced for their eccentric hypotheses, the arrogant ego of the queen is in evidence. Loyalty to royalty does not mean that we have neither our own intellectual authority nor the right to question or oppose the authority of others. Yet that can happen to us when the archetype of queen is overly emphasized. Then we become pawns of power, not sharers in it. This inequality is toxic to the human spirit, the only spirit that can incarnate the Spirit of God. *Hierarchy is the shadow of the queen archetype and the shadow of power in all its forms.*

The dark side of the queen archetype also appears in the loyalty she may demand of us. We may be so possessed by her sway over us that we believe our personality has to die in her service. We may feel it necessary to surrender our uniqueness, our exuberance, or our freedom. A spiritually authentic surrender includes choice *and* self-assertion. Once we trust that the divine life is within us, we are no longer self-abasing. We realize then that incarnation means self-realization. It is not blind and blank obedience. We are cabinet members, not lackeys. We join with the queen in her procession through time; we do not lie down as the carpet she walks on.

The dark side is not malicious. It appears when it is ignored or projected so we can get back on track. It is a signal to find balance when we have become one-sided or are in denial of the potential in any reality—including God—for error or for extremism. The shadow side of the queen, like all shadow energy, thus ultimately helps us find our voice and our power as co-creators, co-redeemers, co-workers in the evolution of love, wisdom, and healing in the world.

> *My knowledge is so weak, O blissful Queen,*
> *To tell abroad thy mighty worthiness…*
> *Guide thou my song.*
> — GEOFFREY CHAUCER

Prayer

O Mary, Queen of Heaven and Earth, I serve you with all my powers and gifts.

I show everyone in my life and in the world around me your royal road of love.

May your presence in my life help me let go of my ego with all its arrogance and with all the fear that drives it.

May I depose that empty power in favor of the real power in life which is to place my gifts at your service.

I offer myself as completely as I can in this moment.

I want to be sent on whatever mission you may have for me.

I want to be a courier of your gentle and guiding love in
    the world.

Rule my mind with wisdom when I am overcome by
    confusion.

Let my mind be a conduit of your truth.

Rule my body with clear purpose when I am at the mercy
    of untamed impulses.

Let my body be the instrument of your freedom.

Rule my soul with healing when I am depressed and
    forlorn.

Let my soul be the channel of your joy.

Rule my heart with love when I am afraid to love freely.

Be the queen and guide of my soul.

Chapter 4

The Mystical Titles of Mary and of Our Souls

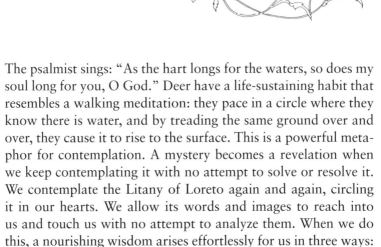

The psalmist sings: "As the hart longs for the waters, so does my soul long for you, O God." Deer have a life-sustaining habit that resembles a walking meditation: they pace in a circle where they know there is water, and by treading the same ground over and over, they cause it to rise to the surface. This is a powerful metaphor for contemplation. A mystery becomes a revelation when we keep contemplating it with no attempt to solve or resolve it. We contemplate the Litany of Loreto again and again, circling it in our hearts. We allow its words and images to reach into us and touch us with no attempt to analyze them. When we do this, a nourishing wisdom arises effortlessly for us in three ways: we discover the qualities of the divine feminine; we realize that the titles of Mary describe our inner Self; we find the multiform graces that they promise and provide. We are in an All and are that All.

Such grace is what has accounted for the appeal of the litany over the centuries. The titles of the litany are the realizations of saints, and they reflect the deepest truths in our collective being. At that depth, we are one with those who have preceded us and linked to those who will follow us. That continuity is the communion of saints. This is not news but a confirmation of an inner and ancient certainty about the vastness of our human heritage. It is comforting to know that our deepest intuitions are shared by saints, sages, and mystics. Sages, in fact, are simply those who have enunciated aloud the collective wisdom of the ages in striking, poetic, and memorable ways. The full spectrum of spiritual knowledge is indelibly in every one of us, no matter how silent or secret. Our psyches are channels of wisdom like nature and like scriptures.

In fact, full consciousness is not the single experience of a single person. For humans, consciousness is an interrelated field. It is interactive, happening in concert with the consciousness of others. This is an implication of the doctrine of the Mystical Body of Christ. Spiritual truths are comforting comrades because they come from the same place in us where there is only one of us. The Sutras and Bibles of all the ages meet and are summarized in the archetypal oracular wisdom of our linked souls, and no accidents or ravages of history can dispossess us of our heritage. Each of us is a holograph of the entirety of revelation. Scriptures as dogma are external, but as archetypal indications of the breadth of the psyche they are part of our internal world and much more powerful since they are part of us.

The titles of Mary in the Litany of Loreto are the many names of our souls, the tongues of Pentecostal fire always above our heads. We invoke Mary to arouse and activate those energies in our daily life. In other words, the litany is a plea for incarnation. It is a blueprint of the feminine archetype in our collective psyche, an outline of our destiny to form/co-create and to transform/co-redeem the universe.

Images are to the mind what instincts are to the body, innate directions toward fulfillment. There are images unconjured by the mind that transcend consciousness and arise spontaneously from the unconscious. These are revelatory gifts of the soul since the soul is a treasury of images. The soul is our organ of spiritual intuition as the mind is our organ of thinking. The soul is our ground of identity and the bridge connecting our inner life to the world around us. In fact, it is soul that makes these two realities one.

The titles of the Litany of Loreto are spontaneous images arising from the collective soul of religious consciousness. Jung says:

Images are able to unite feelings or experiences that seem compelled to battle in relentless opposition in the ego's world. The religious need longs for wholeness and therefore lays hold of the images of wholeness offered by the unconscious, which, independently of the conscious mind, rise up from the depths of our psychic nature.

The titles of the litany create a unique vision of the soul by summoning up a variety of feminine qualities. Our destiny is to incarnate all streams of gender energy into a lifetime of love. This love will look fatherly and motherly, brotherly and sisterly, spousal and platonic, friendly and inimical. Attention to the litanies of Christ helps to balance the Litany of Loreto. That same balance is what we are called to achieve by work and prayer and receive by grace.

Our Personal Path and Calling in the Litany

The ultimate vocation of the human race is in fact one, and divine.　　—Vatican II "The Church in the Modern World"

There are three levels of potential in the human psyche—psychological, spiritual, mystical. These correspond to the phases of our spiritual development: the liberative way, the illuminative way, and the unitive way. The path begins by releasing ourselves from the burdens and obstacles in our psyche. Our psychological work is here. Then we open ourselves to the light of higher consciousness. Our spiritual practice is here. Mystical union follows as a gift. All three phases are a heroic journey of letting go, opening up, and sharing our gifts with the world. Psychologically that is individuation and spiritually it is sanctity.

The contrast between unconditional love and scanty generosity becomes apparent when our fear-based ego encounters the essential Self. Divine Judgment is a universal metaphor for that interior experience. The ego senses itself judged as inadequate and feels the need for purification. Once the purification has happened, enlightenment can occur. This may be why the illuminative way follows the purgative way in mystical prayer.

Mature religious consciousness is thus not possible without three paths: psychological growth, spiritual progress, and mystical union. The psychological path shows us what helps us become healthy human beings and have more effective relationships. Spiritual progress means letting go of an inflated ego and becoming compassionate. Mystical union cuts through dualisms to release the divine spark in us and in the universe and acknowledges them as one and the same. It is interesting to note that a mystic experience is one in which the sense of time and place disappear. This is precisely what happens to us when we find our true calling. We are absorbed so fully that we lose track of time! Our calling is the work that makes us transcend the moment and be in it fully at the same timeless time.

It takes many years to plumb the truths of faith. We imagine at first that they tell of a God far from us and different from us. Then gradually we realize they are about our calling to find and act in accord with the divine within. The traditional truths held in the repository of faith contained this realization. The Trinity, for instance, held the blueprint of how evolution was to proceed in each of is. To say we are made in the image of God is to say we are here to co-create (hence Father), to co-redeem (hence Son), and to co-love (hence Holy Spirit).

To say that we honor the archetype of Mary within ourselves also presents a threefold challenge. Our calling is to be intact and whole in honor of her virginity, nurturant of others in honor of her motherhood, and powerful in effecting world change in honor of her queenship. These three have the dark sides we explored in chapter 3.

We can know our calling only now and here. Honoring tradition means preserving what relates our past resources to our present needs. Part of this process is updating and redesigning traditional practices and beliefs to fit changing needs. This includes a religious sense that is also a politically liberal sense. That is a crucial feature of our calling. To have grown beyond our past is the best sign that we are being guided in the evolutionary process. David Tracy writes: "To disown the reformatory impulse at the heart of tradition is also to disown the Church's apostolic memories of the message, actions, and fate of Jesus. It is to disallow that subversive and dangerous memory of Jesus in the Church. . . . At their best, religions always bear extraordinary powers of resistance. When not domesticated as sacred canopies for the status quo nor wasted by their own self-contradictory grasps at power, religions live by resisting."

The invocations in the Litany of Loreto are bugle calls that rally our soul to its full calling. Some blow taps to ego fears and attachments; some blow reveille to the heart that is ready to awaken. Each title is a sound-bite that launches us on a train of prayer, feeling, and imagery that can lead to charitable action, spiritual awakening, and mystical union—our destiny on earth as it is in heaven. Each title offers a step that can lead to a shift. Each is an acorn awaiting our contemplation of it so it can bloom into a reliable oak of support for our life purpose.

These invocations have the power to enlighten, encourage, console, disturb, and challenge. They accompany us and feed our soul, enlivening us with wise tidings that attend to interior heralds that call us to our full stature. The litany is the product of the Self as it attempts to describe its own magnitude. Our calling can be dangerous. Those who do not understand can say of us what they said of Jesus: "This man has made himself God."

Yet it takes a lifetime to come to full consciousness of just how wonderful we really are. We may know in the abstract, but only gradually does it become concretely acknowledged. St. Cyril of Alexandria wrote: "We have admired his goodness in that for love of us he has not refused to descend to such a low estate as to bear absolutely everything about us, including our ignorance." Jesus knew fully who he was only after the resurrection. This is a metaphor for how we finally know our own divinity, in a resurrection, a moment in which we arise as a Self from the ashes of ego. We are here on earth not because we were born but in order to be born. We invoke Mary as a mother because we know at some deep level in our souls that she can help us be born. Like our death, birth has not happened fully yet. We invoke her also at the hour of our death because we know this too. Such a prayer is not new to human consciousness. The ancient Greek Orphic death-resurrection ritual says: "I have entered the bosom of Persephone, Queen of the Underworld." This is a way of acknowledging the necessity of return to the Divine Mother for rebirth, as we also return to our Earth Mother in preparation for resurrection.

Our calling to virtue is to strip the ego of its inflated status in our decision-making and to allow an ego-Self axis to flourish instead. In Jungian psychology, this is individuation, a fulfillment of our potential to incarnate the virtues of the Self: love, wisdom, and healing power. It is an enterprise that is never finished, always in progress. It is a synergistic combination of effort we achieve and grace we receive. Our ultimate goal is to articulate through our life story—with all its talents, gifts, mistakes, shadows, and errors—the eternal life of the Self and to bring the world along. This is co-creation, the work of incarnating a divine life in all humanity. We each fulfill ourselves in community. We find our potential by participating in the human enterprise, not by standing apart or by competing for the top.

We are drawn into being by a voice that beckons us to incarnate the divine Self. This happens by a combination of choice and grace, symbolically masculine and feminine forces. The call is from within since God is precisely that Within, the depth of our psychic life. A call is a gripping incentive that impresses the ego into the service of higher consciousness. In other words, our human limitations are upgraded when they are humbly surrendered to a higher purpose than the ego's favorite sports: fear, attachment, greed, and control. We then can hear the inner and irrepressible call to be whole. Until then there abides in us an ineradicable longing to fulfill our evolutionary destiny and thereby complete the program for which our unique personality was designed.

An alchemical process can occur whereby the leaden ego is transmuted into the gold of the Self. Our ego and our body are the stuff of the divine work of peace and compassion on earth. The response from us that sets all this in motion is *yes and go,* the combining of surrender and choice, the two responses of Mary at the Annunciation. It is a deft interplay of the impregnating Spirit at the Annunciation and the encouraging Spirit of Pentecost. We stay to be filled with God and we go to fill the world with God.

Mechthild of Magdeburg wrote: "In a dream vision, I saw all of humanity marching toward God, each at his own pace." The timing for all this is unique to every individual. A ship is certainly safe in port, but it was not built for that. It is perfect as a ship but not complete as a ship until it sails. There is a time for sitting and waiting for the wind of grace and a time for turning the wheel with effort.

St. Teresa solved the dilemma of surrender vs. quietism and choice vs. activism by saying it was necessary to let go only when the timing is right for it. She used the metaphor of gardening: Beginners can draw water from a well only with great effort. This is the style of action. Later comes the use of a waterwheel and turning the crank. This takes less effort, as in the prayer of quiet. Third, the water comes directly from the spring, and we simply direct the flow. Now God is the gardener and we the cooperators. Fourth is the stage of union when water simply comes to us from rainfall. We are the receivers of grace in accord with its timing. The time spiritual progress takes is not within ego control but resides in a force greater than ego yet ever accompanying it as the angel Raphael accompanied Tobias with just the right healing balm at just the right time.

The ambition of God for us is probably far greater than any of the ambitions we have for ourselves. It is nothing short of divinity and we have seen images of that all our lives. We mistakenly thought such images presented a great division between us and the divine beings they portrayed. Actually they were simulacra of the Self we were meant to become once our faith was strong enough. We are ready now. Our calling was never anything less than the whole life of Jesus and Mary from the Annunciation to the Ascension and Assumption. The images we venerated were mirrors of our inner life: a heart on the outside beaming love in every direction, a virgin pregnant with God, a piece of bread that can nourish the world, an empty tomb that opens to the light.

We contribute to the upkeep of our soul when we live out the titles of the Litany of Loreto through prayer and practice. They and all the titles of Mary describe the divine life that is the deepest reality of ourselves. Like Mary, we are all kindly parents, mediators of grace, incorruptible, co-redeemers, conceived without sin, nurturers of the universe, ready for assumption into the heaven of the Self. The Litany of Loreto is a list of our callings and our gifts.

The gifts in our healthy ego are unique to us, and the gifts in our higher Self are common to all of us. We realize gradually that our calling, what gives us bliss and purpose, is actually a metaphor of our deepest identity. This concept is stated by Fra Mauro, a sixteenth-century monk and cartographer: "Gazing at the map...all the diversity of the world is intimated on the parchment, even as diversity is intimated within me. The map and myself are the same."

Abbess Hildegarde of Bingen in 1147 A.D. wrote:

I am that supreme and fiery force that sends forth all living sparks. Death has no part in me, yet I bestow death, wherefore I am girt about with wisdom as with wings. I am that living and fiery essence of the divine substance that glows in the beauty of the fields, and in the shining water, and in the burning sun and the moon and the stars, and in the force of the invisible winds, the breath of all living things. I breathe in the green grass and in the flowers, and in the living waters.... All these live and do not die because I am in them.... I am the source of the thundered word by which all creatures were made; I permeate all things that they may not die. I am life.

My calling is ultimately to name myself in many more ways than one. I am David from New Haven in my ego identity. At the same time I am being itself. My intrinsic nature is the essential Self of the universe. My existential body is 5'9″ and 150 pounds and diet can change it. My essential body is pure light and nothing can change it. I am of double parentage: Louise my mother here and Mary my mother Here/Hereafter. This is what Jesus meant by: "Your names are written in heaven." From now on, I will have to give my full location, not found on my driver's license, if the angels are to find me.

While writing this book I had what I consider a rather profound dream relating to the theme of a calling. I was in a barracks facing a woman student of mine, both of us sitting on a cot, cross-legged—a meditation posture. She asked me this question: "What is the space around the world?" I answered: "It has two meanings: one is referred to in the Book of Revelation." She nodded knowingly as I said this. I began to quote Jesus' words: "Behold, I stand at the gate and knock, and if anyone hears my voice and opens the door to me, I will come in. . . . " She gave an indication that she knew the rest of the quotation. "The second meaning of space," I then added, "is pure *possibility.*"

When I awoke I savored the dream as a gift. I felt I had received a blessing, perhaps even a revelation. The contrast between that rude setting and the sublime question and answer gave a clue that in this dream I had entered the spiritual realm. It seemed that I was facing my feminine Self there. My spontaneous—and hitherto utterly unknown response—contained a pointed challenge. I seemed to be finding out that the space in nature—and in my life—is a knock at the door of my soul, a calling, and that what awaits me is something infinitely possible.

> *Do that which best stirs you to love.*
> —St. Teresa of Avila

Mirror of Justice

It was prophesied that the Messiah would be called "The Lord of our Justice" (Jer. 23:6). Mary is the Mirror of Justice because she personifies the divine life in its feminine dimension. A personification has a mirroring quality. In Jungian psychology the anima, the soulful feminine archetype, serves a mirror function in the psyche since consciousness arises from reflection. In the depths of the psyche is the God archetype, and that includes Mary as the female mirror image of the male side of God.

This is all a metaphor since the divine is not caught in human dichotomies and has no sides, only energies that continually interconnect. *The divine is the life in us that transcends divisions.* At the Incarnation Mary found a Source *within,* i.e., she is the mystic who mirrors God as the interior life of herself. When we humans look for God we discover that our souls are mirrors of divine life. When we see God we are finally looking at ourselves.

"Mirror mysticism" was prevalent in the thirteenth century. St. Clare, speaking to Princess Agnes about Christ, said that he was a "mirror without blemish.... Study your own face in that mirror in prayer. Place your mind before the mirror of eternity, place your soul in the brilliance of glory, place your heart in the figure of the divine substance and transform your entire being into the image of the Godhead itself through contemplation." Thus prayer means access to the vast space/inner place within where we are what we pray to. It is looking into a mirror that reflects our essential Self without ego blemishes.

This mirror metaphor is not new; it is a feature of mature religious consciousness the world over. We find a similar concept in Hinduism on the feast of Vishnu. The ritual for that day recommends to the devotee: Close your eyes and direct your face to the altar. When you open your eyes, look into the mirror. You will see not yourself but your mother or grandmother, who will say: "Repeat your mantra, and when you open your eyes and look into the mirror you shall see God." This ritual strongly resembles a dialogue of St. Teresa: "Who are you?" Jesus asks. "I am Teresa of Jesus. Who are you?" "I am Jesus of Teresa."

Mary, as the feminine in divine life, is also a mirror reflecting wholeness, i.e., sanctity. The liturgy for the feast of the Heart of Mary sings:

She is the brightness of eternal light, the unspotted mirror of God's majesty, and the image of his goodness. She is a breath of the power of God, a pure emanation of the glory of the Almighty, hence nothing impure can find a way into her. She is a reflection of the eternal light, untarnished mirror of God's power, image of his goodness. (Wisd. 7:25–26)

The metaphor of a mirror evokes images and imaging. Archetypal images are mirrored to us in litany titles as well as in religious figures, people, events, imagination, art, intuitions, and dreams. Interestingly, in this context Jung says: "Dreamwork releases an experience that grips or falls upon us as from above, an experience that has substance and body such as those things which occurred to the ancients. If I were to symbolize it, I would choose the Annunciation."

To let an image speak to us is thus a path to spiritual vision. This receptive style of imagining does what sacraments and rituals do. It lets us see through the existential literal reality of daily life to the essential mythical reality of the universe/Self. It is a mystical reality we participate in rather than merely observe. In fact, it is precisely through our imagination that we participate in the ongoing creation of the world: "He made them in his own image," i.e., *imagined* us and our world. We continue that creative process prayerfully when we use our imagination as a spiritual practice. Appendix Three gives an example of this.

Imagination is a mirror of images. The titles in the Litany of Loreto arouse imagination because they are words with images attached. "In the beginning was the word." Creation happens from a word spoken to our image-filled soul. In this center, everything in our life and in our feelings, becomes centered, i.e., brought into harmony. To let our imagination be moved by the titles of Mary is a form of prayer to her since the full release of imagination requires a surrender. It is the surrender of ego with all its tried and trusty weaponry: attachment to logical left-brain thinking and rigid mindsets that configure the world in limited and fear-based ways. We believe our minds are less when we think, but we can imagine and let them be more. All great changes and advances began in the imagination—as did every title in the Litany of Loreto.

Imagination, a feminine power, is to the soul what thinking is to the brain. Imagination looks into things to find a personal truth since the whole truth reveals itself in the objective and the personal, one mirrored reality. To receive that revelation and to abide in it is what is meant by transformation. Imagination is thus the ability and skill to see the fullness and unity of human and divine reality as mirrors of one another. Jung believed that imagination was the key to transformation because by it we summon into consciousness what was hidden in our unconscious. Indeed, transformation is always waiting for us where apparent opposites show themselves to be related as complementary, that is, as mirror images.

Imagination is the nature and activity of the soul, the point of meeting between the ego and the Self. Novalis uses this mirror analogy: "The soul is the meeting place of the inner and outer worlds. . . . It is the point at which they overlap." Images are thus the mirroring links between the microcosm of ourselves and the macrocosm of the universe. Images do not forge a connection but expose one that has always and already been there, or rather here. The process of imagination has a spiraling trajectory, from vision to word to deed. We see a better world; we affirm it into being; we act in ways that make it happen. This is how we move from image to action and become a mirror of justice in the world.

The dark side of the mirror analogy is in our tendency to be seduced by images so that we lose our grounding in the here and now. That can distract us from direct contact with the reality of our own commitment to justice. We can be lost in imagination and not move into activation. Our calling is not simply to know of our unity with the divine. Mystics who found that out automatically became more socially conscious, more committed to loving. St. Teresa called her great rapture a mirthful event unless it was followed up by "a life of love lived now." The shadow side of this title is in its potential for too much emphasis on reflection. It becomes integrated when it leads to a plan of action for the evolution of the world. Then reflection becomes restoration. That is how the mystical mirror becomes a mirror of justice.

> *Let us make humanity in our image, in our likeness . . .*
> —Genesis 1:26–27

> *We see now through a glass darkly but then face to face.*
> —1 Corinthians 13:12

Prayer

Mary let me reflect your love into the world.

I want my soul to resemble yours so I give to others what you give to me: a secure feeling of being loved.

May I care about justice so that I act honestly.

May I mirror justice everywhere by standing up for truth as you give me the light to see it.

May I speak truth to power and not be afraid to take a stand for justice.

May I take the part of those who are too weak to defend themselves.

May all that I do, say, and feel reflect your light into any dark time, your concern into any self-centered time, your love into any terrified time.

I am thankful that I am a mirror of justice in the world reflecting your presence and your caring.

I am your mirror, Mary.

May I restore the world to wholeness by my commitment to justice here and now and ever after.

Seat of Wisdom

The word wisdom in Hebrew is *hokmah*. Wisdom in Greek is *sophia*. Both are feminine nouns. *Logos* is a masculine noun. *Logos* and *Sophia* are complementary. Jesus is the Word as well as the Wisdom of God who "became flesh and dwelt among us." Jesus is a personification of the divine Self in all of us. Sophia is an ancient symbol of light and a traditional reference to Mary too.

In a letter to Freud in 1912, Jung writes that Sophia is the same ancient wisdom that is found in depth psychology. This is a way of restating our thesis in this book that the divine life personified by Jesus and Mary and our inner soulful life discovered in the depths of our psyche are one and the same life—and this life animates nature too. Aurobindo says that the Absolute Being has three dimensions: transcendent, cosmic, and individual—and that humans have the same three, a trinity within. The equation is: human is to divine as it is to nature. These are not static energies, but dynamic ones, hence, developmental psychology, evolutionary nature, and process theology. Mary is a personification of the feminine in all three as Jesus is of the masculine.

Archetypes manifest themselves as images and personifications, a given of consciousness. The anima is the soul energy that in its positive aspect is Sophia and in its negative aspect is the destroyer personified in ancient times as Lilith, Kali, or Medusa. The destructive feminine is personified in Greek myth by the witch Medusa, who turns arrogant men to stone. She halts and disempowers the male ego—as Judith does to Holofernes in the Hebrew tradition. This is the theme of transience into mortality. The positive movement to immortality, on the other hand, is personified by Sophia, who raises consciousness and widens human life. Wisdom is thus a mediator granting access to the divine. The shadow, the Judith energy, is ultimately an assisting force since it frees ego of its headiness and finds a way to make it useful to the community.

Mary holding Christ in her arms at Bethlehem is the kindly mother. Mary holding the body of Christ at the foot of the cross presides over the painful dissolution of his mortal life. She brings him to life as co-creator. She assents to his death as co-redemptrix. She holds all of us in both those ways from birth to death and all our lives. Thus she presides over the light and the dark of life. In both instances she holds Jesus and us as the throne, the Seat of Wisdom. The wisdom is the realization that our destiny is both to be comforted and to be crucified. Wisdom is the Holy Spirit that restores us to life and makes us co-creators and co-redeemers. Once Christ is our elder brother and Mary is our mother, their destiny is ours. As long as they are distant divinities, the condition of separation still presides and the Fall goes on.

Sophia is the *Shekinah* in the Kabbalah. The *Shekinah* is God present among us, canceling distance. Jung wrote:

> When John [in the Apocalypse] pictures Jerusalem as the bride, he is probably following Ecclesiasticus. The city is Sophia, who was with God before time began, and at the end of time will be reunited with God through the sacred marriage . . . the sacred marriage, the marriage of the Lamb with his Bride, which had been announced earlier, can now take place. The Bride is the new Jerusalem coming down from heaven.

There is a continuity in ancient tradition that females were the mediators of archetypal wisdom. We see this personified in the priestess at Delphi in Greece or in the Sybil in Rome. Both had associations with serpents, symbols of resurrection, creatures that would become equated with the demonic in patriarchal teachings. The Christian Bible is the only scripture in which the divine feminine powers are specifically absent or disparaged. The emphasis on one God in the Judaic tradition is not only a way of preserving monotheism. It is just as much an exclusion of the feminine principle in divinity. A reading of chapter 44 of Jeremiah, for instance, shows the ferocity of the priestly caste against the mother goddess as Queen of Heaven. The priests could not accommodate the feminine in the divine.

The goddess in ancient times was joined in sacred marriage to a bull, a symbol of male power. In medieval times the bull became the horned devil, and witches were thought to be his consorts. The alternative ancient sacred marriage image and ritual of the goddess and the king, i.e., the Self and the ego, is a symbol of the ego-Self axis. The sacred marriage of Yahweh and Sophia or of Christ and the church are healthy instances of this in mature Judeo-Christian traditions.

Jung offered a powerful comment on the occasion of the definition of the Assumption in 1950:

> One could have known for a long time that there was a deep longing in the masses for an intercessor and mediatrix who would at last take her place alongside the Holy Trinity and be received as the Queen of Heaven and the Bride of the heavenly court.... It has been known from prehistoric times that the primordial divine being is both male and female. But such a truth can eventuate in time only when it is solemnly proclaimed or rediscovered.

Wisdom is not in logic but in vision and intuition. Our intuition is an expanded consciousness. Building a richer intuitive sense is a life-long work that takes ongoing cultivation:

To look with love amplifies our intuition. A mother's intuition is an example.

To look with no bias and expecting nothing but a surprise makes an intuitive realization more likely.

Humor is a direct path to intuition. When we do not take things so seriously, we are more likely to access cosmic wisdom. Intuition rewards the useful misbehavior of an excess of merriment.

Intuition also comes from bodily resonances and strong feelings. These are evoked by the invocations in the Litany of Loreto, and in that way it can facilitate intuitive wisdom.

Compassion leads directly to intuition: we see the light in order to bring the light into our world.

Most intuitions arrive unbidden as graces, but it is appropriate to request one in prayer or in a dream. We can also communicate with nature and ask for an intuition from a flower, the moon, a butterfly.

Intuitions come more frequently when we listen to them just as letters come more frequently when we answer them.

Mary can be imaged as the personification of the wisdom in every human soul. We see an example of how this refers to God and nature too in Proverbs 8:22–31:

> *The Lord begot me, the first-born of his ways, the*
> *forerunner of his prodigies of long ago;*
> *From of old I was poured forth, at the first, before the*
> *earth.*
> *When there were no depths I was brought forth, when*
> *there were no fountains or springs of water;*
> *Before the mountains were settled into place, before the*
> *hills, I was brought forth;*
> *While as yet the earth and the fields were not made, nor*
> *the first clods of the world.*
> *When he established the heavens I was there, when he*
> *marked out the vault over the face of the deep;*
> *When he made firm the skies above, when he fixed fast the*
> *foundations of the earth;*
> *When he set for the sea its limit, so that the waters should*
> *not transgress his command;*
> *Then was I beside him as his craftsman, and I was his*
> *delight day by day, playing before him all the while,*
> *Playing on the surface of his earth; and I found delight in*
> *the sons of men.*

Prayer

O Mary, throne of wisdom, enlighten my path.

Increase my openness to intuitions.

May I find the wisdom that is in nature, in scriptures, and in my soul: all one truth.

May I share wisdom generously.

May I bring the dawn of consciousness wherever I go and not become lost in the sunset of ignorance.

Free me from prejudice and limitation in my views.

Make me open to all possibilities and intuitions in me, in others, and in the world.

I seek your wisdom in God, in nature, and in myself, and I find your wisdom everywhere.

You occupy the throne in my inner kingdom, and I am always listening to your wisdom in words, in others, in nature, in my soul, and in everything.

Speak your wisdom in ways I can best hear. Free me from deafness to the many voices of wisdom that surround me so beneficently.

Let my intuitions be messages from you.

Give me the gift of caring deeply that everyone find your wisdom.

Give me the gift of sharing the good news with others.

Cause of Our Joy

With mourning and lament I sent you forth but God will give you back to me with enduring gladness and joy.
— Baruch 4:23

The Irish have a devotion, ascribed to St. Thomas of Canterbury, called the seven comforts of Mary. The devotion consists of seven Hail Marys to share in her joys on earth: the Annunciation, the Visitation, the Nativity, the Epiphany, finding Jesus in the temple, the Resurrection, and the Ascension. Mary asked St. Thomas to add seven Hail Marys for her joys in heaven: she is honored above all others; she has purity above the angels; her light illumines heaven; earthlings honor her as the mother of God; her Son grants what she asks; she can and does give grace; and her glory increases till the end of time. These are qualities of the soul of humanity and of nature too.

All these joys reflect the themes that have characterized devotion to the Great Mother throughout recorded history. Mary is the cause of our joy by her participation in the history of our salvation, prefigured in the Gospel and occurring in real time now when we are saved from bondage to the limitations of ego.

The themes of bondage in Egypt and of exile in Babylon are two central motifs in the Hebrew Bible. Bondage brings the grace of liberation. Exile ends in homecoming. Both are occasions of joy. The idea of a spiritual journey is the background of both themes. Exile is the metaphor for the alienation that happens when we become stuck in our own needs and desires, separate ourselves from others, and imagine God to be far and away from us. Bondage is the metaphor of being caught in the staring face of ego: fear, attachment, control, and entitlement. Joy results from freedom and homecoming. Mary is a guide to these possibilities since all her joys flow from her combining choice and surrender.

Mary is also the cause of our joy because she brings Jesus into the world for us. Theologian Edward Schillebeeckx wrote: "Being sad in Jesus' presence was an existential impossibility." (We are in that presence now right here inside us.) Jesus is the new Moses who joyously leads us out of our bondage in ego into the promised land of the vast inner Self. Mary is the cause of our joy because she accompanies us on that spiritual journey.

The Hindu mystic Ramakrishna wrote: "The Mother does not love those who just float out into the transcendent. The Mother really loves those who play the game wildly, who go for it." Throughout the centuries the worship of the divine mother was an uninhibitedly joyous experience. One way this

was maintained throughout Catholic history was by the folk rituals surrounding Mary as the Queen of the May. The singing,
the crowning of her image, the festive atmosphere open us
emotionally, another passageway for archetypal energy.

Joy is not limited to fun. It can be a quality of any experience.
A rose faces autumn with a joy equal to that felt in spring. She
knows she will be reborn though not as this same individual
rose. Her joy is precisely in the fact that she is not attached to
an identity in any limited or literal way.

The shadow side of joy is in the intruding recognition of the
momentary nature of all experience, a built-in variability in the
conditions of existence. Since the archetypal Mary is nature, that
is part of her shadow. To say yes to the givens of life is devotion to her. That yes helps us since by it we let go of our ego
attachment, the most inveterate obstacle to authentic joy. This
is the joy of equanimity in the midst of shifting predicaments
and shifting feelings in a shifting world—what is meant by joy
in suffering. We then not only accept things as they are; we savor
them. The dark side of joy is that it ends. The light side of it is
that we fight endings tooth and nail only to find that they help
us grow and move on. The shadow proves to be our ally once
we befriend it.

Does this mean we are not to have feelings, to weep for losses,
to react to the tears in things? There is a story about the Zen master Shaku Soen. He wept for a man who had died, and his tears
were ridiculed by a bystander who said: "Are you not supposed
to be beyond reaction to the conditions of existence?" Shaku
answered: "It is this allowing of grief which puts me beyond it."
Feeling is not opposed to the yes or to a "Thy will be done." It
is an adornment of it.

We are creating ourselves moment by moment through the
dark and light of relationships, events, feelings, images, and all
the phantasmagoria of human life—what Dante calls "the little
threshing floor that makes us all so ferocious." The soul does not
care about the price we may have to pay to arrive at spiritual
individuation. If it takes dissolution, that is accepted. If it takes

a long silence, that is endured. If it is blessed with rapture, that is gladly welcomed. Joy is an ingredient of any day in which wholeness can unfold, and that is everyday.

Mary is a personification of a sanctity that may happen in us in a variety of ways: sanctity is in letting go of an ego that is caught in fear and attachment in favor of an unencumbered and loving ego. That is joy. It is in articulating and incarnating in daily ego life the abiding powers in the divine Self: love, wisdom, and healing influence—the same qualities we have revered in Christ and the saints. That is joy. It is in receiving the graces that make all this possible. That is joy.

The rendezvous of ego and Self is painful when we fight it but bliss when we welcome it. Contact with the Source of human inspiration within—the Self—is friendship with ego. *Enjoyment can become our motivation in the spiritual life.* There is a long-standing connection between reverence and humor. Compare these two quotations from the Hebrew Bible: "He fell on his face and did reverence..." (2 Sam. 9:6). "He fell on his face and laughed..." (Gen. 17:17). Can we picture Christ or Mary laughing? If we cannot, our image of them—and of sanctity—is stunted.

Mary is the cause of joy *because* she is full of grace, the free gift of spiritual energy and momentum that complements our work and shows us the divine potential in ourselves. The cause of joy is in us since wholeness and sanctity are in us, the God within. Teilhard de Chardin wrote: "Joy is the infallible evidence of the presence of God." Wholeness is another name of God. Since our life purpose is to be holy/whole as God is holy/whole, our destiny is one of joy. Our religious experience in the church may have been humorless. It is time to restore the joy of the saints, the whole ones, to our spiritual life. Mary's joy today is in the activation of joy in us here and now. This is how we may add one more heavenly joy to the ones she listed for St. Thomas of Canterbury. It is also how we become saints.

The archetype of the divine feminine is eternal. It is the true cause of a human joy that beckons to us from the beginning of time and never ends. That joy is our best motivation for virtuous acts. In spiritual maturity we are not good because we are bullied by a fear of punishment. We are good because we are full of delight.

> *Now all good things come to me together with her and*
> *innumerable riches through her hand and I rejoiced in all*
> *these.*   —Wisdom 7:11

Prayer

O Mary, you are the cause of so much joy in my life and in the lives of my ancestors.

For this I thank you.

I am grateful for the joy of liberation from ego.

I am grateful for the joy of saying yes to what is.

I am grateful for the joy of my spiritual practice.

You are the Source of joy and the miracle of joy-in-pain.

May I find ways to hold those two in my heart as one.

I cherish the memory of your many joys on earth and in heaven.

I see them as promises of what my life can be.

Joy happens when I love with all my might.

Joy happens when I give myself passionately to my destiny and forget myself.

Let these joys happen in me.

May I bring joy to the world as you did long ago and as you are doing now.

Vessel of Spirit

Mary held all these things within her,
pondering them in her heart.
—Luke 2:19

Mary is called a Vessel of Spirit, a Vessel of Honor, and the Singular Vessel of Devotion. These titles were added to the litany in medieval times when alchemy was popular. Alchemy was not about transforming lead into gold literally. The vessel in which the leaden ego is transformed into the gold of the Self is the spiritual enterprise behind the primitive chemistry. In Tibetan Buddhism, the peacock is the symbol of the bodhisattva because it was believed that he ate poisonous plants and transformed them inside himself so that they became his colorful plumage. It was believed in medieval times that the peacock was a symbol of resurrection, that its flesh was an antidote to poison.

In the metaphor of the alchemical vessel we encounter the two maternal themes of forming and transforming. Mary is the vessel for the gestation of the divine incarnated as Jesus and then as all of us. She is also the spiritual vessel in which opposites combine: the painful process of letting go of ego occurs so that the golden Self can appear. In Buddhism, Maitreya, the bodhisattva of love, is pictured holding a vessel containing the waters of enlightenment. He waits to baptize the world until it is at its worst ebb of delusion and violence. Only then is the world ready for its transfiguration. This is another way of seeing how light dances with shadow so that harmony can result.

Vessels contain elixirs and love potions which are also symbols of transformation, often with dark overtones. In fact, the stories of witches and potions were always about a spiritual rebirth, never literal except to those not in the know. A witch is a personification of the negative side of the anima, the female force that dissolves ego and transforms us in a painful initiatory way. This is the shadow of the vessel archetype. To form and contain is a tranquil gift of the good mother. To transform is terrifying because it is challenging, instigating, moving, life-changing, and compelling. Mary is not the opposite of the witch but includes her energy. In medieval times when witches were burned and Mary was glorified, Mary was being burned too.

Mary has been honored as the good mother and witches have been perceived as evil women. Now the full archetype has to be located in Mary. She is too powerful a figure in the imagination of humankind to be cut in half. We can welcome her as the chthonic shadow mother, the feminine transformative heft in nature. What was the province of witches and sirens is now to be restored to Mary. The positive and negative are two energies in one continuum, and Mary is the archetype that can contain them. This is a recognition of the power of the feminine to embrace the variety of human experience and its destiny of transformation.

In Athens Venus was venerated as the goddess of love. In Sparta Venus was the goddess of war. The dove is sacred to Venus in her love aspect; the sparrow is her bird in her lust aspect. This is not contradictory but an intelligent recognition of the full expanse and interchangeability of an archetype. The Hindu pantheon also reflected unity in diversity. Heinrich Zimmer writes of the beneficent divine mother *and* of the destructive mother Kali as "the dark, all-devouring time, the bone-wreathed Lady of the palace of skulls." This is not meant to be a horror but a metaphor of the cost of evolution, the cost of spiritual development, the cost of discipleship. We become whole in the life of Christ the same way he did: we are born of Mary in Bethlehem and are held by her at Calvary as our sufferings are transmuted by grace. She forms and transforms us by our own devotion to her. When we honor her and venerate her, she works in our lives in joyfully creative and painfully redemptive ways.

Something feminine abides as a transformative energy in us, always at work in grace and action, and that is what we have known all our lives as Mary. There is a synthesis of dark and light in the process of transformation. Thus mother nature both feeds us and poisons us with mushrooms. Waters may drown us or slake our thirst. Earth is our origin, and that dust is later what our bodies become. Earth feeds us throughout life and a hungry earth eats us at death. These are metaphors—like the litany titles—of a human reality and a divine destiny that thrive in light and dark.

The theme of this title is containment. Mary is the vessel of safekeeping and incubation. She is the baptismal font of new life. She is the holy grail that contains Jesus/us. Mary contains divinity like a pyx, a word derived from *buxis,* box. She is the tabernacle, what St. Paul called a "vessel of election." In Judaism the tabernacle is womb-like and contains all of God's revelation, which is nonetheless continually unfolding. It is not a binder of old canonical texts but a releaser of new and never-ending visions.

The divine mother has also been symbolized as shelter in caves, sanctuary in a cathedral, a *temenos,* the sacred space for formation/creation and transformation/redemption. These are ways of declaring her power of containing us and reforming us as we pass through this vale of tears and joy. It is also a way of affirming that we are continually held, that we are not alone or simply out there. We live within, not outside.

A vessel is also parthenogenic since change happens within it while it is sealed, like a seed in the earth. This is another pointer to the spiritual meaning of Mary's virginity: The consecration of a baptismal font includes these words: "May a heavenly off-spring, conceived in holiness and reborn as a new creation, come forth from the stainless womb of this divine font." Virginity is not meant to refer to physical but to spiritual intactness in the midst of all the vicissitudes of human transformation. It is a metaphoric mystery, not a literal reality.

"To whom much is given much will be required" (Luke 12:48). To fulfill ourselves as unique human beings means manifesting our talents and finding our bliss. This is the way our unique life and gifts become the intact vessel of divine life. It is an incarnation of the universal in the unique. "Everyone of you should know how to maintain his vessel in sanctification and honor" (1 Thess. 4:4). How that can happen is summarized in the invocations of the Litany of Loreto and in these meditations on them.

Mary is called the Singular Vessel of Devotion. Singular in Latin is *insigne*, i.e., eminent. "Devotion" is from the word for vow. Our destiny is to be vowed to or consecrated to the twofold graces of Mary: to allow her to form and to transform us in her own way. To be in the vessel of election is not to be in control of how it works but to allow grace to have its way with us no matter which exigencies we may have to deal with as part of the process. Mary is the archetype of grace because the feminine brings grace into our lives so copiously.

We are not only the receivers of graces but the mediators of them to others. We co-create the earth by our faithful love for it, and we redeem it by our unconditional love. This can only happen through humility since "we carry this treasure in vessels of clay, to show that the abundance of the power is God's [the Self] not ours [ego]" (2 Cor. 4:7).

> *Even though we are small vessels,*
> *you have filled us.*
> — MECHTHILD OF MAGDEBURG

Prayer

I live my life in the vessel of your love, O Mary.

You contain me and all my feelings, my thoughts, my fears, my hopes, my sufferings.

You are the elixir of change and growth for me.

You transform my leaden ego into the gold of love and higher consciousness.

You burn me when necessary and reconstitute me.

You crush me and make me the best wine for the wedding of all humankind.

You are the crucible in which a great change is happening in me.

May I remain loyal to this process, however painful it
may be.

May I emerge from it with an enduring commitment to
encourage those who are afraid of the fire.

May I remain devoted to you and make my contribution
to the evolution of the universe through all I receive
from you.

O Mary, keep pondering me in your heart.

Mystical Rose

The alchemical and baptismal theme meets us again in this beautiful invocation. It comes from Sirach 24:18: "I was exalted like
the rose of Jericho." That flower is still sold there today. Roses of
Jericho are actually dry tumbleweed that bloom rose-like when
placed in water. They are transformed once they are contained in
water, like us at baptism. They thus also summon up the alchemical image of the dark side of the anima: the sirens who dissolve
the ego in water so that a spiritual consciousness can emerge.
Holy water has this same significance. We sign ourselves with it
upon entering a church to transform head, heart, and shoulders
from the ego world to the world of the eternal Self.

Goddesses have perennially been associated with flowers. The
rose in the Hebrew Bible probably refers to a crocus or saffron;
hence it is red in the Song of Songs. The blood-red color makes
the rose a symbol of resurrection and gives scars and death a
mystical significance. This is why roses are placed on graves.
Flowers are intimately connected to the dark side of life, i.e., its
movement toward death.

The Mystical Rose can also be a lotus, the symbol of spring,
which grew in the Jordan valley in Bible times. Astarte figurines
found there show the goddess holding a lotus. The Buddhist
Mother Tara holds a lotus stem with three branches in her left
hand representing her three concerns: past, present, and future.

Her right hand is open, giving blessings to humanity. Buddha is pictured as the jewel in the lotus, the Eastern counterpart of the rose. The lotus rises from the primal muddy waters. This evokes the alchemical theme of perfect beauty from ugliness, another symbol of the light and the dark in one archetype.

The rose is the Western symbol of wholeness and it is also like the virgin, whole and intact, a flower unfolding. The Cosmic Rose in the Hindu tradition is meant to describe the beauty of the divine Mother. The rose is the mystic center of perfect and unsullied sanctity. The rose window of a cathedral is a mandala of wholeness, a window to another world beyond the ego's narrow and limited vision.

Dante wrote of Mary: "Here is the rose wherein the word of God was made incarnate." He uses the image of the white rose both for Mary and for the beatific vision. This is another reference to Mary as a mediatrix, a character of the middle world between heaven and earth and combining them. Heaven is an image of the Source and destiny of the psyche. It too is a rose that combines the feminine light in its blossoms and the feminine dark in its thorns. Where the variations are united, a spiritual direction is being taken. (It is a touching synchronous fact that a group of courageously ingenuous and idealistic young people in Nazi Germany formed a resistance movement, for which they were all martyred, called "The White Rose.")

Angelus Silesius in the medieval poem "The Romance of the Rose" sees the mystical rose as a symbol of the soul and of Christ's action upon it. The Golden Rose blessed by the pope on the fourth Sunday of Lent symbolizes his spiritual power. Thus the mystical rose shows the spiritual power of the Self in which we all participate.

The Rosalia was a pagan ritual that took place in May—later to be Mary's month—when roses were offered to the dead. Hecate, the goddess of underworld—the dark side of the anima—was sometimes depicted with a crown of roses. The "Grateful Dead" uses this same ancient symbol of roses on the head of a skeleton. In recent times roses are also a symbol of love with all its thorny vicissitudes, another metaphor for the alchemical transformation that can happen only in and through the shadow.

After his vision of Mary at Tepeyac in 1531, Juan Diego was asked by his bishop for a sign. Roses sprung from rocks and were gathered in his cloak along with a picture of the Madonna, Our Lady of Guadalupe. Mary was appearing on the spot where formerly there was a shrine to the Aztec goddess who presided at that very place, even wearing her same colors. This fits with our vision of Mary as the great mother cherished everywhere throughout history. Apparitions are visions of the Self granted as cheering graces to the ego along its mortal path. The Mary who visits the world in apparitions is the archetype of the bodhisattva, the enlightened person who keeps coming back to earth to help others find the light. Unfortunately, the verbal messages of the Madonna in the apparitions reported in the twentieth century have often been fear-based or have fostered superstition. This reflects an unhealthy atmosphere that has prevailed in the church and in the world. The new milieu is one of openness and discovery. Perhaps Mary's messages in this new millennium will be more encouraging and life-affirming.

The rosary uses the word "rose" because the five petals of a rose in medieval times signified Mary's five joys and the thorns her sorrows. The rosary combines three mysterious roses, white, red, and gold. The white rose is joy. The red rose is sorrow. The gold rose is glory. The joyful mysteries of the rosary are in the leaves of the rose. The sorrowful mysteries are in the thorns. The glorious mysteries are in the petals. They thus each connect with nature. In addition, all fifteen mysteries concentrate on the bodily experiences of Jesus and Mary. The rosary is a chain that links the spiritual with the natural and the physical, another reference to the middle world. Its popularity reflects the wisdom of the psyche: the recognition of how human nature and the divine nature are united. Our Lady of Lourdes, the goddess as healer, appeared with a white rose on one foot and a gold rose on the other to show her twin concern with earth and heaven, another joining of the human and the divine.

On January 18, 2000, while working on this book, I was graced with a visionary dream. I dreamed that a student asked me if the world was getting worse. I said: "No, it is only that its shadow is becoming more richly revealed. It is a mystical rose that is opening and we are seeing more deeply down into its dark petals."

Prayer

Rose of all my life, I trust you with my past, present, and future.

You are the promise of a renewal in my life that begins today and will cycle throughout my future.

You are the flower of opening and the flower of closing.

You bloom in my heart and I can feel myself expanding.

You bring the thorns that help me become stronger.

You show me how to accept the cycles of change.

May I trust the changes that happen and grow through every one of them.

May I bring the rose of you to everyone I know.

May I lose my ego by taking refuge in the opening rose of divine life.

May I find the mystical rose in my heart, in nature, and in all my fellow humans.

May I bring the rose of you to all who wander in this garden and may not notice its blooms.

Be the gardener of what next will bloom for me.

Make me a rose that opens to the world, mystical rose.

Tower of David, Tower of Ivory

A tower is a middle world, a symbol of the connection between heaven and earth, that is, between the ego and the higher Self. The roots of a tower are deep in the earth/nature, and thus all three worlds are united: natural, divine, and human.

The tower of Babel was meant to be a ladder to heaven to repair the broken tie between humans and God. The tie is the axis of the ego and the Self that can be restored when people let go of hubris and practice the virtue of humility. Instead Babel became a symbol of the inflation of the ego and so led to division and disconnection, that is, sin, isolating ourselves from love both vertically and horizontally. Grace is in the combination of surrender and choice for an axis with the Self. Sin is the combination of surrender to ego and the choice of ego instead of an axis with the Self, i.e., instead of a life of love, wisdom, and healing.

To apply the image of a tower to Mary reflects a long-standing belief in the human psyche that feminine energy has a restorative dimension. It rebuilds the severed unity within us. The tie between the human and the divine cannot be truly broken since the divine is the deepest reality of the human psyche. The tie is broken only in the sense that we are no longer conscious of it. This is why enlightenment is not something we seek but is already the case with all of us. We do not become enlightened; we simply notice it at last. That consciousness is not a choice as much as a grace, and thus it is a feminine archetype.

Towers were common in the biblical landscape. They were made of brick or stone and were used for refuge from or for defense against armed attack. A tower was a citadel for the whole village (Judg. 9:51; Ps. 61:3; Hos. 61:4). Towers sometimes contained wells and were used for the storage of harvests. They were refuges for sheep and workers. Some were military strongholds in the walls of the city for safety during a siege. This symbology of containment and protection was easily applied to Mary in medieval times. She is not only a tower in the sense of connection but in the sense of refuge and safety.

In Christian times the tower was also a symbol of watchfulness and ascent. Towers are observation posts. They take solar energy and distribute it on earth. This is symbolic of a rise in consciousness. Mary is the model of this since her combination of surrender and choice brought a higher consciousness to earth. Jesus is the personification of that consciousness, and we are the heirs of it. We are the present-day children of Mary with a messianic purpose: to bring love, wisdom, and healing into the world through the formative and transformative energies of the feminine.

Mary and Joseph are from the family of David, and Mary stands out like a tower since she forecasts the arrival of a messiah. "Your neck is like the tower of David, built with elegance; on it hang a thousand shields, all of them shields of the valiant" (Song of Songs 4:4). This refers to a specific fortress built by David, who had recaptured Mount Sion from the Jebusites and built a tower there. The Tower of David was prominently visible to the inhabitants of Jerusalem. From it warnings could be broadcast if enemies were approaching. By King Herod's time only the foundation remained, and he built three towers on the site. The strongest of these was called the Tower of David. It survived the destruction of Jerusalem by the arrogant Roman general Titus, a personification of ego that destroys the temple of the Self. The tower of David was impregnable against the foe, as is the Self to the arrogant ego.

Stored in the spiritual tower is the weaponry we need to sanctify ego: virtue and grace. The military image of arms and armory fits. Once we activate goodness—Godness—in ourselves we find ourselves up against the collective shadow: "Our wrestling is not against flesh and blood, but against principalities and powers, against the world rulers of this darkness, against spiritual forces of evil on high" (Eph. 6:11). It is dangerous to be a saint.

Mary is compared to the Tower of David because she is part of a divine defense system in our souls. In her the Kingdom of God (the world of the Self) will stand undefeated, and sin (the choice to succumb to the shadow of ego) will be conquered. Hubris is believing only in the masculine effortful ego and denying its counterpart, the feminine energy of grace. Grace is required in letting go of ego. It is a gift that does not originate in us. This is how grace can make for a change from arrogance to gratitude.

A tower is a container, the locus of formation. This also makes it a fitting symbol of the divine mother. This archetype appears again in the Song of Songs: "I am a wall, and my breasts are like towers. Thus I have become in his eyes like one bringing contentment" (8:10). This contentment and containment are the dark side of the tower archetype. It can prevent us from finding our wanderer energy, our warrior energy, our courage in direct engagement with life's challenges. When Mary becomes a refuge, her shadow appears and we can be lost in it. Our calling is to know when to enter the tower and when to stand outside it.

The image of the Tower of Ivory further shows the feminine side of the archetype. This term is used in the Song of Songs to describe the beauty of the beloved bride: "Your neck is an ivory tower" (7:5). Psalm 45 images the bride of the Messiah in an ivory palace filled with music: "From palaces of ivory, harps entertain you."

In the Hebrew tradition, the Sabbath is referred to as a bride. In some rabbinical texts the creation occurred precisely *for* the Sabbath. It was not God's sabbatical but his purpose. The feminine archetype represents a purpose of humanity and of nature: to stand out like a tower and be a reliable refuge in a world of illusion and distraction. It is not a sanctuary of stone but of soul. It is not granted to us because of our efforts or merits but because we are loved by a Love greater than ego:

> *It was not by swords they won the land;*
> *It was not by their arms they gained the victory;*
> *It was by your right hand, your arm*
> *And the light of your face*
> *because you loved them.*
>
> —Psalm 44:3

Prayer

> O Mary, on earth as you are in heaven, restore the connection between heaven and earth.
>
> Show us heaven on earth as you showed your Son to humanity.
>
> Heal the separation that has happened to us:
>
> Let us find divinity in our humanity and in nature.
>
> Be our citadel against the powers of evil that rise against us.
>
> May our love transform them and bring out the love in them, a love that is real but now hidden by fear.
>
> Be our support in times of stress and neediness.
>
> Be our refuge when we are attacked and misunderstood.
>
> Help us stand outside the tower long enough to find our strength.
>
> Support us with the strength to face what life brings and not to lose heart.
>
> Support us with an armory of love and peace.
>
> May we become your peacemakers.
>
> May we go out into the world and stand out as towers for those who need us and may we become liberators too.

House of Gold

I remained . . . in the temple, enjoying the ineffable pleasure of contemplating the goddess's statue, because I was bound to her by a debt of gratitude so large that I could never fully repay her.   — APULEIUS

Mary is what we are: a temple of the divine. In this title we have two symbols, the house as a container and gold as the supreme value of the Self. The house of gold is the Self. A house grants shelter so we again encounter the conserving and containing aspect of the female archetype. It is comprised of the light of comforting safety and the dark of numbing contentment. There are always graces to help us integrate those two.

The Loreto shrine, the traditional house of Mary, is like the Ark of the covenant, the dwelling of the feminine aspect of God. At sunset it is bathed in gold, and so it is often referred to as the golden house. It has been visited by pilgrims since medieval times including Sts. Ignatius, Francis de Sales, Charles Borromeo, and Alphonse Liguori.

A house, be it a hut or a castle, is symbolic of the center of the universe, the Source and the goal of the human journey. St. Teresa wrote: "Consider our soul to be like a castle made entirely of diamond . . . in which there are many rooms. . . . If this castle is the soul, *clearly one does not have to enter it since it is within oneself.* How foolish it would seem if we were to tell someone to enter a room he was already in." This is a remarkably clear reference to equivalence of the divine Source and the essential Self. What a contrast between the diamond soul of St. Teresa and our first introduction to the soul as stained by sin!

A house appearing in dreams is thought to represent the human psyche and body. Ania Teillard says that in psychoanalysis a house signifies the layers in the psyche. The exterior of the house represents our persona, our outward appearance, both our body and our personality. The floors are the layers of consciousness in us, and the stairs are the connections between them. The attic is higher archetypal consciousness, and the cellar is our roiling unconscious and instincts. The kitchen is the place where food is transformed by cooking so it can become a source of nurturance. This is an alchemical symbol of the changes we are capable of when our ego is burned away so the Source can work through us. The doors represent our openness to the world and our passages in and out. Through them we move from contemplative silence to active work and universal charity.

This description from depth psychology is a richly spiritual view that shows how a house is an image carefully and usefully lodged in our consciousness to show us the dimensions and potentials of our true selves. As a title of Mary, a house serves that same purpose. She is the house of human psyche with all its exits and entrances, its ascents and descents, an allegory of a possibility in our life for divine incarnation. We are the house in which the transformative mother is at work. Our task is to allow that housework to happen no matter how hot the kitchen may become or how many stairs there are to climb. We are never alone in the house; our mother and our spiritual ancestors are at home with us as coworkers and sponsors.

In 1 Kings we find this reference to Solomon's temple: "There was nothing in the temple that was not covered with gold... within and without" (6:22). At its dedication God promised to hear the prayers uttered in it. Mary as mediatrix of graces is the archetype of the golden temple in whom prayers are surely heard.

Gold was common in ancient times since it did not require the use of metallurgy to process it for use. It is thus symbolic of the pure Self that does not require the interventions of ego. It is thereby also a symbol of grace and of spiritual virginity. Gold in India was called "mineral light." Gilding of images of gods and saints was meant to show their spiritual perfection and how they hearken from a world beyond ego. Byzantine icons were gilded to reflect light from heaven. Halos are gold auras betokening the divine light that emanates from saints who are incarnations of the divine life.

Images of gold appear throughout the scriptures. In the Apocalypse, the new Jerusalem is a symbol of the Self since it was made by God as opposed to the ego version made by man. It is made of gold: "The city was built of pure gold, like polished glass" (Rev. 21:18). Gold is likewise a gift of the Magi, a gift of the wider world to the ever reborn Self that is always embracing the world.

There is in this title, as we are seeing in all of them, a shadow side. Gold is associated with greed and miserliness. Gold can tempt us to sell our loyalty. Gold also can be *tried* as in Job: "He has tried me as gold that passes through the fire" (23:10). This house of gold of the spiritual Self stands in contrast to the golden house built by Nero, a personification of the ego, after the fire he set in Rome in 64 A.D., a house of vanity, which was itself destroyed soon after. The persecuted Christians whose numbers increased would build a city of God in its place. After the conflagration of ego desire comes the house of gold of real value, that is, of an essential truth. This is the painful dimension in the story of human transformation.

A custom in our American past was to bronze the shoes in which a baby first walked. Mary is the house of ego that has been gilded because she walked the path from ego to Self. She represents the completed process of the ego-Self axis. By the invocation House of gold we commit ourselves to enter the mansion of spiritual individuation. What happened to her happens to us: we make a series of choices and surrenders that move us from cellar to attic and then down to earth and out into the world with treasures to share. This passage will have suffering in it and joy too, like all human enterprises that say yes to the inexorable conditions of existence. That yes to golden light and bronze darkness is what makes for incarnation.

> *In the fire of creation, gold does not vanish: the fire brightens. Each creature God made must live in its own true nature; how could I resist my nature, that lives for oneness with God?* —MECHTHILD OF MAGDEBURG

Prayer

Mary, we enter the house of your golden radiance.

We find in you the virtues that make our world a house of gold.

We share with you the house of earth and join you in making it a palace of light.

We offer the sunrise and the sunset to you.

Help us in our beginnings and our endings.

Give us strength to face new possibilities.

Give us strength to face our griefs and trials.

We are always at home in your love and ask to stay with you through all the seasons of our life.

May we make the world a house of golden love.

May we grant hospitality to all those we have turned away.

May we create a home on earth that welcomes all people.

May our goodness be visible by what we include, not by what we exclude.

Mary, you are our home, and we are your home.

Thanks to you, no one and nothing is left outside.

Ark of the Covenant

The Ark of ancient times was a container, hence a feminine symbol: "In the Ark was a golden vessel containing manna, the rod of Aaron that had budded, and the tablets of the covenant" (Heb. 9:4). The Ark was made of incorruptible wood, a symbol of the deathless Self. As we saw above, the word *Shekinah* is the Hebrew word for the Ark, connoting the feminine presence of God.

The Ark of the covenant was the pledge of divine protection, so it was taken into battle. The Self is our protection in our battle with ego. The Ark is related in the Litany of Loreto to Mary's role as the mother who holds and preserves our intactness in the face of the threats of the inflated ego. The covenant is the promise that the ego can enter the service of the Self accompanied by the Self and sanctified by it. When the Israelites fought without the Ark in their ranks, they were defeated. This is an allegory of the need for grace (feminine energy) as a supplement to effort (masculine energy) in opening ourselves to the establishing of the ego-Self axis, i.e., union with God.

As the Israelites crossed the desert to the promised land, a cloud, signifying the presence of God, "overshadowed" the tent containing the Ark. That same word is used in the Annunciation story: "The Holy Spirit will come upon you and the power of the Most High will overshadow you" (Luke 1:35). Mary contains Jesus in her womb as an Ark. She accompanies us as an Ark, i.e., by containing our divinity.

This is not a limited literal concept but a rich allegorical reference to our universal destiny as humans. These images are not proofs that Jesus is the messiah who abrogates the Hebrew Bible covenants. Nor does it follow that Jesus is the messiah and no one else is. Jesus as messiah is the personification and exemplar of our universal human purpose to be co-creators and co-redeemers. These images are out for higher stakes than to show how Christianity fulfills Judaism. They tell of how we are all called to fulfill our evolutionary goal of bringing unconditional love, enlightened wisdom, and healing power into our world. It is not about preparation for a heaven in the future but a commitment to a new heaven and a new earth here and now. *In fact, this is why we are here now.*

The three covenants of Judaism are those with Abraham, Noah, and Moses. The covenant with Abraham signifies the promise that God, the essential Self in all of us and in nature, will remain alive in every generation. The covenant with Noah is that of the preservation of life until an omega point of evolution when a triumph of spirit will become visible in the material world. The covenant of Moses makes all of us a chosen race to bring the law of love to fruition. All three of these promises require masculine efforting and feminine containing for their fulfillment; hence the Ark is such an apt image and symbol.

Hugh of St. Victor saw the Ark in an allegorical way. He referred to it as the Ark of the Heart. It is the secret core of the body that is the equivalent of the Holy of Holies in the Temple of Jerusalem. It is the secret container of wholeness that awaits the gifts of divine grace and the work of human effort to be released. The heart/ark is also the alchemical vessel in which the base metal of ego is transformed into the gold of the essential divine Self. In this context it has been associated with the Holy Grail, another symbol of wholeness, in which natural life force, wine, becomes the divine life force, redemptive blood. This is the shadow side of the image: the suffering that is necessary in the process of transformation.

Jung compared the Ark to the female breast that gives nurturance and the treasure chest hard to find in which is stored the wealth of wholeness. He also sees the Ark as a metaphor for the sea that receives the setting sun and brings it to birth again the following morning. In this sense it is a symbol of the reliability of resurrection.

The Hymn for the Office of Our Lady of Lourdes shows the dark and light dimensions of all this when it sings: "The torrent with its inauspicious waves which draws all men [egos] into the whirlpool subsides into a placid sea [the Self] while the Ark of the covenant [feminine presence] is passing by." This is a reference to the dark Red Sea that awaited the Egyptian soldiers (the arrogant ego refusing rebirth) and dissolved them. That same sea will be one of light and will baptize and liberate the ego ready for an axis of power with the Self.

All these references allude to other titles in the litany and show the ultimate unity of all of them as an affirmation of the meaning of Mary in our spiritual lives. We can see the Litany of Loreto as a necklace of pearls that have value singly but together create a stunning marvel of spiritual adornment and inner wealth. The invocations ornament us and enrich us because they cull so many provocative metaphors about our spiritual path and what it takes to walk it.

"The temple of God in heaven was open and there was seen the Ark of his covenant" (Rev. 11:19). This is a way of confirming that these images signify celestial archetypes of the Self. The Ark is a heavenly figure since it is a container of the divine.

The personal ego world cannot hold such a tabernacle; only a transpersonal world can. The Ark, like Mary herself, is transcendent and unlimited. In Ecclesiastes we read: "He who made me rested in my tabernacle" (24:12). This is why Saturday is Mary's day: God rested in her. She is the Sabbath, the feminine divine, and so are we when we grant hospitality to our feminine energies.

Meditation on a daily basis is conducive to releasing feminine energy. Exodus 31:17, an account of creation, says: "God rested on the seventh day and watched his breath." The word *nafash* means to rest or breathe, and *nefesh* is the human soul or spirit. Both these words are from the same root. So the breath of God is a metaphor for the soul at rest. The soul is feminine and so is the Sabbath of rest. Since mindfulness meditation involves watching our breath, it is thus a direct contact with divinity, the essential Self beyond ego. In the Kabbalah, the highest level of the human soul is *neshamah*, the breath of God. The lowest level, the soul in us, is *nefesh* and what connects these is *ruach*, which means breath both as respiration and as the life force, the axis of the divine and human soul. This is the meaning of Pentecost, an allegory of how the humbled ego becomes the mouthpiece of the good news.

The Catholic parallel to mindfulness is "the prayer of quiet regard" in which we look at something in nature with no interpretation or interfering mindsets (fear, desire, judgment, expectation, etc.). We take a deep breath and simply witness the reality before our eyes while letting it speak to us. This is a way of contacting the lightness of being, finding the transpersonal in the natural. It is indeed a mystical connection between the human, the divine, and the natural. We look at an it and it becomes an I, as Jesus said, "Be not afraid, it is I." We make Light of it.

As the Ark arose, so on this day the virgin mother was taken up to her heavenly bridal chamber.

—St. Anthony of Padua in a sermon
on the feast of Mary's Assumption

Prayer

Mary, you keep the divine life in safe-keeping for all of us.

You, not my ego, are my protection in times of conflict.

Let me dance in your presence.

Keep a covenant with me all my life.

You are here today accompanying me on my journey.

I feel your guidance and appreciate it.

Mary you contain all my past with its long history of light and dark.

You contain my present with its fears and longings.

You contain my future with its mystery and surprise.

Hold all these in your heart.

Carry me in you as you carried Jesus.

Carry me as the Ark carries the presence of God.

Be the holy grail to me, the wholeness of my mortal and immortal life that nourishes me in ever more marvelous ways.

May I be the presence of the divine in my home, at work, in the daily world and in all that I do.

May I be a tabernacle of nourishing and exuberant love.

Let me rest in you and awake in you.

Gate of Heaven

A gate or door is a symbol of a passage into a new world or a new state of consciousness. Opening gates means opening a new knowledge to us and granting us access to the world of grace. That knowledge is the realization that what we believed in as literal all these years was containing and preserving sacred metaphors about the destiny and identity of our psyche. To walk through is to forsake literalism and polarity for a courageous consciousness of who we really are. The Litany of Loreto is a map of the far and inner-flung territories of that indestructible Self. All the titles describe what is true of us at the level of soul. We are those who pass through the gate, and we are the gate through which revelation passes to the world.

The transit to the new revelation is only for those who can leave ego behind with all its F.A.C.E. of fear, attachment, control, and entitlement. Therefore at the temple gates are guardians who may frighten us. We are asked to face a painful initiation. We see in the guardians the shadow side of the feminine. As always, that shadow is not malicious but probative and assisting. The minatory feminine is protecting us from getting in too deep when we are not yet ready. If we cannot pass the guardians we certainly are not equipped for the greater storms of life that follow. The guardians of the gate are the shadow side of the givens of life that try our patience and our courage. They also symbolize entry to the unconscious, always a frightening prospect for the ego.

These are the main givens we humans were given: things change and end; things are not always fair; our best-laid plans oft go wrong; suffering is part of growth; people are not always loving and loyal. These givens are actually the gatekeepers of spiritual awakening. This is how nature is the dark side of the feminine powers. The givens of human nature hurt us and try us *while* they make us stronger. They are a product of growth and a price of growth.

Paradoxically, if we can deal with the givens, however harsh, by saying yes to them and by not quarreling with them, we win entry to a realm beyond givens. That realm is the state of equanimity, the nirvana or heaven of letting be. The conditions of existence are then not simply painful givens but also the escorts to character, depth, and compassion: If our deepest reality is divine then the conditions of existence are divine graces since they give us depth, which is precisely where we find the divinity in ourselves.

Most prisoners of war suffer for years in reaction to what was done to them. The Tibetan Lamas who are tortured by the Chinese are not afflicted later with post-traumatic stress syndrome. Their spiritual practice over the years prepares them for any predicament that may occur in the drama of the human shadow. Their devotion to their faith and their trust in karma makes them impervious to torture, since they are free of blame or hate or retaliation. The Christian martyrs surely achieved that same victory. A spiritual practice thus contributes not only to our sanctity but to our sanity.

A gate has a threshold, an archetype of protection and challenge as we enter a world beyond the one we are in. Through the gate we pass from the profane world to the sacred world, as happens when we enter a cathedral. Mary is the gate through which Jesus—divine consciousness—entered this world. Mary is the middle world gate through which we enter the sacred world of spiritual consciousness.

Christ is our exemplar of the human incarnation of the divine: "the firstborn of many brothers and sisters." To say he is the door is to acknowledge that this transition is achieved not by ego but by grace. Jesus says: "Behold I stand at the gate and knock, and if anyone will open the door to me I will come in to him and sit down with him and sup with him and he with me" (Rev. 3:20). This is the promise, to open the gate and let heaven into earth.

For the Jews, Passover night was considered the time of the Messiah's arrival when the temple gates would open on their own. This is why the early church expected the Second Coming on Easter eve, the new Passover, during which they listened for a knock on the door. Only those who were holy—free of ego fear and desire—would be able to enter (Rev. 22:14; Ps. 118:20).

Mary, in the Gaelic litany, is called Ladder of Heaven. The title Gate of Heaven is taken from Genesis: "Indeed the Lord is in this place and I knew it not. How terrible is this place! This is none other than the house of God and the gate of heaven" (28:16). Jacob said this the morning after his vision of the ladder connecting heaven and earth and trafficked by angels. The theme of ascent and descent, from ego to Self and Self to ego, is likewise a covenant image. Access is always and everywhere available to the ego to enter the divine life, which so zealously yearns to enter the ego's world.

Gold and precious metals represent spiritual meaning. In Herod's temple, the central gates were covered with gold and the "Beautiful Gate" was covered with brass. Here, while the gate was open, St. Peter cured a crippled man while saying: "Silver and gold I have none, but what I have I give you: Arise and walk." An open gate is significant as a symbol of the entry to the temple of the divine Self. There is a touching and profoundly provocative legend that the parents of Mary, Joachim and Anne, met and fell in love at this same Beautiful Gate.

> *Mary is this eastern gate. For a gate which looks to the east is the first to receive the rays of the Sun. So the most Blessed Virgin Mary, who always looked toward the east, that is, to the brightness of God, received the first rays of the sun or rather its whole blaze of light. This gate was shut and well guarded. The enemy could find no entry, not even a little chink.* —St. Aelred of Riveaux, twelfth century

Prayer

O Mary, help me see, open, and pass through the gate between fear and love.

Show me every day how to reflect and foster compassion, wisdom, and healing.

Be a door for me into the divine life.

Help me say yes to the givens of human life.

May I accept how things change and end.

May I accept how things are not always fair.

May I accept how my best-laid plans may go wrong.

May I accept how that suffering is part of growth.

May I accept that people are sometimes hurtful and
     disloyal, and may I never retaliate but instead pray
     for their transformation.

Teach me to say yes to the givens as the will of God.

Let me find in the givens the sources of compassion for
     others who share them.

Open the gate to your way of loving and seeing where and
     how I can love more.

Open the gate to higher consciousness for me, Mary.

Open the gate of light to Light. Let the light through.

By your grace, may I be a gate of heaven on earth.

Morning Star

Morning is promise and beginning. The red morning star is a
symbol of the rebirth of life as the homecoming of light. This
connection to the theme of birth makes it an apt symbol in the
story of Bethlehem when it led the shepherds and the Magi to
the infant Jesus.

The early church fathers spoke of the "morning star" that
shines brightly before the sun rises as symbolic of Mary the
Mother of Jesus, the Light of the World—the Sun—who preceded his coming. The mystic St. Bridget of Sweden said of Mary:
"She is the star that precedes the sun." Heavenly bodies, the
stars, sun, and moon, are symbols of the spiritual dimensions
of psyche, not earthbound, not ego-bound, but transcending us
while at the same time hovering over us as our custodians.

Mary as the woman in the Apocalypse is described this way:
"On her head was a crown of twelve stars." The hymn for the
feast of the rosary says: "Twelve stars now crown the brow of
the glorious mother who reigns near the throne of her son over
all created things." The stars in her crown are the beacon that
calls us to co-creation. In the hymn for the feast of the guardian

angels Mary is called the "Mother of Light." Our Lady of Light is a medieval title given to her by St. Thomas of Canterbury. That light is the light of consciousness, the abundant potential in the Self once it is acknowledged by the ego, as sailors acknowledge the morning star with joy and a sense of being held, protected, and guided. This fits with a reference of Shakespeare in *Measure for Measure:* "Look, the unfolding star calls up the shepherd." The morning star was the signal to the shepherd to lead his sheep from the fold, that is, to begin another day of giving nurturing care.

The morning star is particularly associated with the sea. Pagan goddesses were associated with the primal waters. Even the Holy Spirit in Genesis is depicted as a mother bird brooding over such waters. The great goddess Aphrodite is born of the sea. The Sumerian goddess who creates heaven and earth has a name that means sea. The name Mary is a cognate of the Latin word for sea.

St. Ephraim wrote: "Mary is the safe harbor of all of us sailing on the sea of the world." The divine feminine has a guiding quality. An old Irish prayer says "O Mary, meet me at the port." The complete Mary combines light and shadow. She is thus both the open sea with its hazards and assets and the port with its comforts—and hazards too.

In Roman times, the guardian goddess Isis was portrayed with a ship. In Buddhism, Tara, the great mother, is the lady of the beasts who pacifies the flood and rescues the shipwrecked. The church is itself pictured as a ship that carries us over "life's tempestuous sea." The word "nave" is used for the main aisle of a cathedral. The image implies containment and safety in the midst of change and upheaval. The eternal Self ferries the ego stably through its many vicissitudes on its voyage.

A few years ago, I visited the childhood church of my grandmother in Meta di Sorrento, Italy, Our Lady of the Laurel. I noticed first a plaque that said it was built on the ruins of a temple of Minerva, goddess of wisdom, an indicator of the unity of the great mother archetype. Meta is a town on the water, and many of its citizens are sailors, my great-grandfather being one of them. In the church I found a wall covered with individual paintings of ships. Each of them was tossing perilously in the midst of nighttime storms. Each showed an image of Mary above the ship. She appeared as a shining starry light granting protection and assuring the sailors a safe passage through the convulsing waves. I found this set of pictures a beautiful and touching example of the local people's appreciation of Mary as the morning star, a symbol of the great mother as the one trusted to show the way home. Shakespeare notes this life-giving side of the anima in *Pericles:* "Divinest patroness, and midwife gentle / To those that cry by night, convey thy deity / Aboard our dancing boat...."

In *The Tempest,* he also says: "Though the seas threaten, they are merciful." This is a reference to the dark side of the feminine and its immediate connection to the light. The great mother is the guide as well as the storm. The conditions of existence include threatening and dark seas, but within that same archetype is the mercy of a compassionate, luminous, and assuring presence. It occurs to me now as I write this that the paintings in grandma's church depicted Mary and the storm within one picture. Perhaps without even knowing it, the artists could not help but include both sides of Mary: storm and safety framed in one scene. They loved her and love made wholeness visible and universal wisdom accessible.

> *Starry amorist, starward gone,*
> *Thou art what thou didst gaze upon!*
> *Passed through thy golden garden's bars,*
> *Thou seest the gardener of the stars.*
> *She, about whose mooned brows*
> *Seven stars make seven glows.*
> *Seven lights for seven woes; ...*
> *When thy hand its tube let fall*
> *Thou found'st the fairest star of all!*
>
> — FRANCIS THOMPSON, "The Dead Astronomer,"
> in memory of a Jesuit astronomer

Prayer

> Mary, you are the promise and the compass for my human voyage.
>
> Be a star on the sea of my life with all its tempests.
>
> Be a calming presence in the midst of the tumultuous waves that often overtake me.
>
> You are always with me.
>
> Let me see you both in the calming of the waves and the rushing of the waves.
>
> Let me trust your dark side that tries me and your comforting side that cheers me.
>
> May I be a light to those at sea.
>
> May I help those who are lost in the waves of greed, hate, and ignorance.
>
> May I be a star not in the worldly ego's way but in a spiritually guiding way.
>
> Mary, radiate your light so that all fears may be dispersed from every human heart.
>
> You are the morning of our life and its evening.
>
> You are the star of our drama and the heroine of our story.

Health of the Sick

"Jesus was traveling all through Galilee ... healing every disease and every sickness among the people" (Matt. 4:23). This power he shared with the apostles: "They shall lay hands on the sick and they shall get well" (Mark 16:18).

Such healing power is a quality of the divine Self in all of us. It is associated with Mary as the feminine aspect of the Self, meaning that it is contained in the feminine and available through the feminine, i.e., by grace. The Latin word for health is *salus,* which also means salvation. Health is lively freedom from the grip of ego and thus indicates spiritual salvation, not just physical wellness. We are always finding higher stakes in the spiritual world. To say that Mary is the health of the sick is to say that nurturant love is a healing force.

St. Camillus, patron of the sick, founded an order to aid the ill in honor of Our Lady Health of the Sick. There is a picture with this title by Fra Angelico in Rome. Pope Pius V prayed before it for the victory of Lepanto in 1571. The work of St. Camillus in the seventeenth century provides us a significant allegory. He was a soldier who was wounded in the leg and it never quite healed. Because of this disability he was rejected for monastic life. St. Camillus did not despair. Instead, he devoted himself to caring for the sick.

Later, he was ordained and founded his own congregation, the Ministers of the Sick. He and his followers worked in hospitals in Rome and Naples. St. Camillus attended plague victims on ships arriving in Rome's harbor at Ostia. The first field medical unit was formed by St. Camillus when he sent men to serve the wounded in Hungary and Croatia. He was canonized in 1746 and is the patron of the sick and of nurses.

A calling is not just about giving to others from our store of gifts and talents. It is also about giving from our wounds. This is how we befriend the shadow side, and it becomes a source of healing light. Our painful wounds become openings for us and for others too. St. Camillus represents this crucial feature of the Christian message: the potential of grace to make our condition our calling. He himself was sickly most of his adult life, but that only served to make him more conscious of the needs of others suffering like himself. St. Camillus is a model of accepting the conditions of one's personal existence and thereby growing in compassion, depth, and character. He was politicized as a champion of the neglected sick by his own incurable illness. This is how he was not a victim but a resource. His illness became the door to his destiny. In other words, both his illness and his charitable response arose from a divine Source.

To say that Mary is the Health of the sick is to say that the same consciousness in St. Camillus is in all of us since we all contain the energy of the feminine archetype. Sickness is not limited to its narrow literal meaning. It means limitation of any kind. All our disabilities in loving and in talents and in vision, all the givens of our existence are meant to be directions to our destiny of giving. We look at our deficiencies and find compassion for others like us. We design an apostolate of works of mercy that are aimed at the people who are suffering as we are: If we are sick, we help the sick. If we are ignorant, we help the ignorant. If we are in an oppressed minority, we join our fellows in raising consciousness.

Like St. Camillus, we do not wait but are always on the lookout for how we can do this. We go to the harbor, as it were, to see if anyone has the plague. We hear of war and send our prayers, our donations, or ourselves to heal the divisions that caused it. We do not do any of this entirely out of our own effort. We receive a call from within and "the help of thy grace" to send us to our task. Loving ourselves happens best when we do not avert our gaze from the suffering of others. This is because a willingness to see suffering engenders compassion, and that makes us loveable to ourselves.

The title of Mary as Health of the sick means that grace is what heals, and we are its instruments. Mary showed us how at the Annunciation when surrender led to grace and choice led to action. We say yes to our condition without protest or blame. We then choose to make it a path to a purpose. That purpose is what we *are* in our deepest reality, an essential Self full of graces. The graces are unconditional love in our hearts, wisdom in our minds, and healing power in our hands and souls. Grace is the source of wholeness.

The fact that herbs have healing power is an encouraging sign that the earth is with us in the enterprise of evolution. Nature, like Mary, is the Health of the sick. "All is medicine" was a revelation to the Buddha as he contemplated the earth. That realization is the same as the one that says that all is divine or all is one. Mystical union is a way of affirming a continuity in the reality of God, nature, and humanity. It is not about approaching a dualistic Wholly Other but about a coherence always and already in all that is.

A moment of tender oneness with a person we love shows us the possibility in immediate palpable experience for this mystic realization. It is a short step from oneness with One to oneness with all. Such union is felt and known only in moments, as in Wordsworth's "a *flash* that has revealed the invisible world." Each invocation in the Litany of Loreto is just such a flash. Teilhard de Chardin says that truth has to appear in only one mind for one moment to become a universal phenomenon that "sets everything ablaze."

The divine mother is the equivalent of this oceanic consciousness spoken of by mystics. Ramakrishna, a nineteenth-century Hindu priest of Kali, the dark goddess, was a devotee of the divine mother. He reports in his diary that once when he was close to suicide, he had a powerful and rescuing vision: "Suddenly the Blessed Mother revealed herself to me.... Everything vanished, leaving no trace, and in their stead I beheld a limitless, infinite, effulgent ocean of consciousness. As far as my eye could see, the shining billows were rushing at me from all sides."

Prayer

O Mary, may my wounds become openings for a new way of loving and living.

Heal me of my blindness when I refuse to see the light.

Heal me of my deafness when I refuse to hear the good news.

Heal me of my muteness when I refuse to speak up against injustice.

Heal me of my lameness when I refuse to walk the path.

Be with me in physical illness so that I find healing.

Be with me in spiritual illness so that I find healing.

May I bring healing into the world in every way I can.

May I heal the environment.

May I heal divisions among people.

May I heal war and injustice.

May all that I am and will be bring healing to the world.

I am open to accessing healing power by commitment to
these four steps:

Gratitude for grace,

Firm conscious intention to release healing energy,

Letting go of attachment to any particular outcome,

Saying "Thy will be done."*

Refuge of Sinners

*The infinite goodness has such wide arms
that it takes whatever turns to it.*
— DANTE

Sin and repentance are corollaries of the archetypal theme of
redemption. Repentance is a return to the Source of love and
forgiveness. The Source is our essential Self once it is free from
captivity in ego. Moral living can be configured as the removing
of obstacles to that Source. Repentance does not mean dis-
crediting or disparaging ourselves but finding the higher Self in
ourselves once we are free of attachment to ego fear and desire.

---

*These are powerful steps toward opening ourselves to the healing possibilities in us
both spiritually and physically. Healing biophotons can be emitted from our hands.
Conscious intention, as in the four steps, is causal and nonlocal. This is how healing
happens even through prayer at a distance.

The mystic Juliana of Norwich wrote: "Sin is behovely [necessary] but all will be well." She taught that sin has no ultimate reality since it is based on ignorance, and yet it does lead to knowledge and thereby it is useful. This is a forceful way to describe the shadow and its creative potential on our spiritual journey. This potential is based on the certainty that there is no retaliation in God, only transformation. The mystery of the divine is that *it makes all well in the end by never giving up on us.* To say that Mary is the refuge of sinners is to say that an energy of acceptance and forgiveness is always present till the last moment of our life, no matter how we have disfigured it or ourselves.

Mary is the refuge of sinners because we can trust the feminine energy in the psyche to show us the way to love and to repent when we have been unloving. Mary as the mother of Jesus loves as he does: by forgiving and reconciling rather than retaliating, by caring for others through the works of mercy, and by an unconditional self-giving.

Sins are deliberate breaks with the community of humankind. These happen by revenge, malice, disrespect for the feelings of others, greed, and trespassing on others' rights. This refers to our interactions with other people but also to our relationship to mother nature. She provides the warmth and beauty that is a sanctuary for us in our sorrows and confusion. It is sinful to disrespect nature and harm her with pollution and a misuse of her resources. We are asked to love the world by finding ways to preserve it, honor it, and amend our ways in it. This is the transition from sin, ego-aggrandizement, to unity, eco-aggrandizement.

Buddhism comments on both the concept of refuges and that of sin. In the Buddhist tradition there are three refuges: the Buddha (enlightened mind), the Dharma (the teachings), and the sangha (the community). These reflect the three refuges in Christianity: Christ, faith, and the church. The Buddha mind is Christ consciousness, a consciousness free of ego. The Dharma is the word of truth, scripture and tradition, that sets us free from ignorance. The sangha is the community of believers we gather with, those who present the challenges and comforts so necessary on our spiritual path. These are not to be construed as male archetypes since they combine male and female energies. The refuges are not meant to be escapes from the conditions of existence. A refuge opens *in* them when we say yes unconditionally to them. The refuge that opens is an unconditioned state in the psyche. This is why the refuge of sinners, like all the archetypes behind the litany titles, is the divine life within us.

The Hindu teacher Nisargadatta says, "Sin is that which binds us." In Buddhism sin is considered ignorance. There is a story of Buddha in which he meets a bandit who says he has no hope of salvation because of all the evil things he has done. Buddha responds by saying that though the ocean of suffering he may have caused is boundless, he can always turn around to see the near shore. That shore is the refuge that appears in repentance. St. Thomas Aquinas, in answer to the question, Can we ever give up on ourselves, says grace is always available no matter what we have done. Despair is therefore never a necessity. We always have a refuge.

All through our childhood we may have thought of Mary first when we felt we had done something terribly wrong. That was an intuitive recognition of what she is and what she offers and wants to be for us. Sin means separation and redemption means reunion. Mary stands under the star of Bethlehem that unites shepherds and kings. Mary stands under the cross and unites those who hurt and are hurt. Mary stands in the upper room on Pentecost and unites all humankind in the good news of salvation. She thus represents the feminine aspect of the divine at moments at which redemption releases its tenderest mercies.

Refuge of sinners is one of the most comforting of all the titles in the Litany of Loreto since it combines the shadow of sin and the light of forgiveness. It thereby confirms the reality of a loving presence that is responsive to us when we are at our worst. We all make choices that are not in keeping with the love that is in us, not in keeping with the wisdom that is in us, not productive of the healing powers in us and through us. Such choices contradict the meaning of our humanity since that meaning is God, and God is the love we at times reject, the wisdom we at times disregard, and the healing we at times refuse to foster.

Sin is thus ultimately a disloyalty to the deepest reality of ourselves. It is going out of spiritual character. Calibrated into our psyche is a conscience that tells us when we have missed the mark, the many-splendored life of God within us. In that same calibration is a simultaneous desire to make amends and to be forgiven. The archetype of Mary as the refuge of sinners stands in readiness for us in that moment. We will perhaps never appreciate Mary enough. We will perhaps never fully notice how she does not give up on us ever. Maybe we will never be fully aware of how much she cares about our life and our destiny or how much she figures into it.

Refuge means container, and this title therefore certainly refers to Mary as a mother. To pray to Mary as refuge of sinners is not just a consolation; it is a way of noticing and honoring the transcendent mother who contains us unconditionally, both in sin and in grace. We do not have to measure up before she will love us; we measure up because she loves us. In a way, any community in which we are loved and forgiven is a maternal container. These are human metaphors that describe the nature of love. It has a motherly forgiving quality. We find that not only in Mary but in our own hearts every time we do not give up on ourselves or others. The refuge of sinners is not some place outside us but a home base. Home is psyche and nature and the divine life. Mary is the guide to homecoming.

Prayer

O Mary, help me let go of my arrogance and practice humility.

Show me how to ask forgiveness and make amends.

Show me the path to repentance and forgiveness.

I turn to you when I know I have done wrong.

You help me make up for it in ways that make me a better person.

You are always with me, loving me unconditionally, caring about my choices, helping me see better choices.

I am thankful for all the times I have felt your presence in times of error and ignorance.

May I be as forgiving to others as you are to me.

May I be a refuge to those who hurt me.

May they find forgiveness in me that helps them change and grow.

May I let retaliation change into reconciliation.

May I let hurt change into healing.

May I let fear change into love.

Comforter of the Troubled

I looked for someone to grieve with me but there was no one; I sought for one to comfort me but there was none.
—Psalm 68:21

A religious community in Spain was founded in 1380 to rescue abandoned children. It was called "The Mount of Pity" under the protection of "The Mother of the Forsaken." It will naturally occur to human imagination to associate pity for children with the feminine archetype. This is why a title like this one is applied to Mary and, it follows, to the feminine in us.

This title takes us to the core of the Christian gospel. Commitment to the good news is not about beliefs, or being right, or being preferred. It is about loving in the most practical and immediate ways. The call, the challenge, and the grace of a spiri-

tual life is commitment to the works of mercy. The bodily works
of mercy are:

> To feed the hungry
>
> To give drink to the thirsty
>
> To clothe the naked
>
> To shelter the homeless
>
> To visit the sick and imprisoned
>
> To assist the dying

In today's world with CNN telling and showing us daily where
and how human needs are crying out to us, *there is no fam-
ine, only genocide*. We see the deficiencies and horrors people
face all over the world and we can choose to join or support
organizations that help them or we can simply switch the channel. The choice is a commitment to acts of mercy or a disregard
that permits the injustice to go on.

The spiritual works of mercy are:

> To comfort the troubled
>
> To counsel the confused
>
> To provide information to those who need it
>
> To speak up to the unjust
>
> To forgive injuries
>
> To bear wrongs without retaliation
>
> To pray for the living and the dead

Each of these refers to an underlying oppression. Redemption
means release from such injustices. In this sense salvation is
always and already happening as long as we are engaged in
the works of mercy in the world. "Redemption of the world is
the tremendous mystery of love in which creation is renewed,"

writes John Paul II. We are thus co-redeemers when we see pain and respond to it with a compassion asserted so potently in the works of mercy.

Three stages may occur in our expression of the works of mercy. At first we are touched by the suffering of others; we wish the best for them and do not add to their suffering. In the second stage, we cultivate the mind of love, working out specific ongoing ways to make a contribution to the well-being of others. In the final stage we are dedicated to a life of universal love. This in Buddhism is the bodhisattva vow and in Christianity is commitment to sanctity. *Which stage am I in at this time in my life?*

Mary's title of co-redemptrix can be applied to all of us who are dedicated to doing this. It is not a diminution of the role of Christ or a displacement of him. It is an acknowledgment of the shared nature of redemption. That task of grace requires male and female resources and is a community experience. The church is not just a community of those who are redeemed. It is the community of humans everywhere who are committed to co-redeem the universe. The works of mercy are a means to that end.

Spiritual practice leads to developing the musculature to hold a wounded humanity as Mary does in the *Pietà*. Our work is to expand our lap and widen our embrace. Our trials in life and its conditions are a discipline, a workout to build this strength. We are children of Mary when her children are ours. That is the unifying love that makes us conscious of others' pain and makes us more apt to heal it. God is love means that we are love in the world.

What does this look like in practical terms? It is a virtuous life: we act with unconditional love, patience, courage, and joy. Humility and equanimity help us acknowledge our occasional helplessness as we accept the things we cannot change or amend. Finally, compassion springs from a felt sense of our shared humanity and leads to the works of mercy.

There is a healing power in this for us. We will find a direct path that takes us from saying yes with equanimity to feeling sympathy with humanity to the joy of personally letting go. We then create a new set of givens in human relating, those of paradise: love, caring, and generous responsiveness to suffering. This is how we co-redeem.

The dark side of being a helper and healer is the same for both this title and the next one. It has to do first with a helper's potential for enabling those in need to imagine themselves as unalterably victimized or incapacitated. Appropriate contributions on the other hand, both psychological and physical, are those which facilitate others in helping themselves. Another dimension of the shadow of helping is hierarchical attitudes; the helper sees himself as above the one being helped. True commitment to bring healing happens in the context of responsiveness to the human condition. All of us need assistance in some way at some time. When others need help, we are there for them. When we need help, we hope they are there for us. Compassion is not hierarchical in any way; it is the encounter of humans in a peer relationship. Real love does not oblige us or advance us. It opens us to our purpose and makes us all equal.

Mother Teresa was a model of comforting the afflicted. She found a way to remain personally centered and serene while at the same time fully feeling the anguish of others. She did this not by alternating between the extremes but by holding them both simultaneously. This is how she literally "held herself together." She held the leprous with respect, not disgust, because in that moment of looking at the sores, she was still in full contact with her loving Source. As D. E. Harding says in his book *Head Off Stress*, "Mother Teresa . . . solved the problem of being surrounded by unbearable suffering by immersion in it, by being it absolutely and not being it absolutely. It is not a case of balancing one thing against the other, of compromise or moderation, but of extremism."

The mature spiritual path is the one that holds an entire spectrum of extremes. On the cross, Christ said "Why have you forsaken me" *and* "I commend my soul to you" in the same hour. This is a metaphor for a rich human possibility to hold the apparently opposing energies of our feeling selves. In traditional theology it was held that Christ on earth was always simultaneously in the heavenly presence of God. This now outmoded belief is nonetheless a way of preserving a truth: we are always connected to the eternal no matter what the circumstances or distractions. That is part of sanctity, i.e., wholeness.

The saints keep appearing as assisting forces and models for us. They are benevolent collaborators who surround us invisibly throughout the day and especially in times of crisis:

> Elisha rose early one morning and went out; and there surrounding the town was an armed force with horses and chariots. "O my lord," his servant said, "what are we to do?" Elisha prayed to Yahweh: "Open his eyes so he can see." Yahweh opened the servant's eyes and he saw the mountain covered with horses and chariots of fire surrounding Elisha. (2 Kings 6:15–17)

We admire certain saints more than others. There is a reason for this. It is because they represent and personify our own untapped potential. *They had and gave the very gifts that are in us too.* Our admiration of others is a clue to a cornucopia of gifts and possibilities in us. One way to know our apostolate in the world is to consider which saints, canonized or not, we most admire. They are the ones to imitate and to invoke as patrons in finding and fulfilling our vocation. Admiration is a gift of discernment. It points to our life purpose, our destiny, and to our assisting forces ever visibly or invisibly surrounding us. *Look around.*

Remembering My Childhood Collection of Holy Cards

Those more than men and women,
Sentries kindly watching out:
Was I perfectly at home at heaven's gate?

There was Jesus, his heart brim-full
With longings for my loyal love.
And, ah, his mother pausing at my fragile heart,
Loving me no matter how many times I ate the apple.

An off-world family album
Of all my ghostly relations,
Each resembling the me I was designed to be:
I too would someday tear into dragonsflesh;
Someday stand betrayed by the arrows of friends,
Someday burn at the stake for no god reason,
And even give away my bread to melodious bobolinks.
I was being groomed to battle Lucifer in Paradise.
I was being winged to escort an orphan across a crumbling
    bridge.
I was slated to bring forth everyone's redeemer.

I will give my body as food;
I will brood over chaos;
I will let light be.

That box of blueprints,
Holy pictures wholly me.

Prayer

Comfort us all, grace-giving Mary, and let me join you in
    comforting the world.

I commit myself to act with mercy in every way I can.

I will look for ways to feed the hungry, clothe the naked,
    and shelter the homeless.

I commit myself to comfort the troubled.

I commit myself to counsel the confused.

I commit myself to speak truth to those who ask it.

I commit myself to speak up to the unjust.

I commit myself to forgive injuries.

I commit myself to bear wrongs without retaliation.

I commit myself to pray for the living and the dead.

May I find the courage to act as Jesus Christ here in my world toward every person who makes a claim upon my love.

> *Add love . . . then wilt thou not be loath*
> *To leave this paradise, but shall possess*
> *A paradise within thee, happier far.*
> —JOHN MILTON, *Paradise Lost*

Help of Humanity

The title Help of Christians hearkens back to the sixteenth century. It is said that Pope Pius V added this invocation to the litany after the battle of Lepanto; but this is unlikely since it first appears after his time. The feast of Mary Help of Christians, May 24, was instituted by Pope Pius VII in 1815. He was arrested by Napoleon in 1808 and released to Rome in 1814 on that day. Years later, in 1868, St. John Bosco, founder of the Salesians, dedicated the mother church of his congregation in Turin to Our Lady Help of Christians. The Salesians have carried the devotion on since then.

The word "Christian" however is too limiting a word in this invocation to Mary. The title Help of Christians has to be opened to include all humanity. Once nonviolence is a spiritual practice, we no longer believe in victory as the triumph of one army over another. Victory happens when war is avoided and peaceful means are found as an alternative. It can never again be Christians against Moslems by war or Christians against Jews by anti-Semitism. There are no enemies in Christ's world of love, a world that began for us during the Sermon on the Mount and never ends. Christianity is a social crisis in world history. Violence has been replaced with nonviolence, greed with sharing, fear with love, and dogmatic slavery with the freedom of the children of God. As Italian social commentator Danilo Dolci says: "By our nonviolent action we shall show that truth has its own strength."

In the Sermon on the Mount, Jesus said: "If someone strikes you on the right cheek, turn to him the left." In the Israel of Jesus' day, official public acts were sealed using the right hand. To hit someone on the right cheek required that the back of the hand be used. The back of the hand was a sign of contempt and disrespect and used for people of lower or no status. The palm of the hand was used between equals. To turn the left cheek insists to the aggressor that the injured person is an equal. It shows the aggressor that he believes he has dignity and will not be demeaned as "less than" others. Thus the teaching includes personal worth and the ending of class distinctions as well as nonviolence in the face of unfair aggression.

We are called to a revolutionary love, one that is nonviolent, nonretaliatory, and nonexclusive. Here is a summary of how Martin Luther King in *Stride for Freedom* outlined the pivotal points of the strategy of nonviolence:

Nonviolence is not nonresistance but nonviolent resistance. This is why it is not for the weak but takes discipline and requires strength.

The purpose of nonviolence is not to defeat or humiliate the opponent but win him over so he can be included in a community of love.

Nonviolence is directed against the forces of evil, not against people, so we despise the evil deed, not the doer of it.

Suffering is not to be sought as a good, but unearned suffering can be trusted as redemptive. The challenge is to transform evil into good through suffering as a skillful means.

Nonviolence is an attitude, not just action. Not only do we not shoot, but we do not hate either.

"Nonviolence," says King, "is based on the conviction that the universe is on the side of justice." We are not acting against the grain but with it, since redemptive suffering is built into nature as in the example of any death of a rabbit so that a brood of eagles can live.

The hero is not the person who conquers others but the one who unites and reconciles them. The heroic journey is an evolution from the solo-operating of the ego to fellowship and interdependence. Such respect for life is the foundation of adult love. Interdependence is the key to caring about others because our own self-interest becomes equal to the interests of others. Compassion becomes unconditional and universal in its reach. That is the reach of Our Lady, Help of Humanity.

Lepanto is about heroes and villains. The hero archetype can become so autonomous that it is only an inflated ego, the shadow side of heroism. Mary is a universal hero and an assisting force to all of us. She plays a crucial role in our finding humility. Becoming saintly is not a ruggedly individual task but a systems task. It happens successfully only when individual will becomes invested in cooperative effort. That happens in concert with any of the many forces of nonviolence and nonretaliation around us.

An example of one of these forces is found in the action of an Armenian community in Los Angeles. April 24 commemorates the 1915 holocaust in which over one million Armenians were killed by the Turks. To commemorate that day, the Armenians give blood at the local blood bank, and it can be used by any citizen, Armenian or Turk. They *choose* to shed their blood as they once were forced to shed it. They give life to those who took it from them. This is a symbolic reversal of tyranny and hate in favor of generous giving. It is also an immensely admirable example of choosing reconciliation over retaliation.

True victory is not of one nation over another. It is the victory of love over hate, of union over division. This happens spiritually at the intersection of interpersonal effort and the assistance of grace. It happens in psychological development at the intersection of personal work and the aid of grace. For the Greeks, the hero was half human and half divine. This is a metaphorical way of describing the axis of a healthy human ego and the higher transcendent Self. The hero combines the effort of the ego, the assistance of allies, and grace from the spiritual Self.

Aid from beyond—beyond the ego's limited skill and capacity—means that a new consciousness allows for a safe conduct across the trestle of conflict, endowing us at last with what was kept from us before, the riches of unconditional love, perennial wisdom, and healing power, i.e., the qualities of the spiritual Self. This is why relationship with the Beloved within is so central to the heroic journey.

A universally revered icon is that of Our Lady of Perpetual Help. It depicts a pious legend that the child Jesus was visited by two angels of truth who showed him the instruments of his future suffering and death. He was frightened and leaped into his mother's arms so quickly that one of his sandals began to fall off. Mary held him in the safety of her embrace but did not dismiss the angels with the thorns and spear. In the picture we notice that Jesus is held in such a way as to be able to see the givens of his life *and* still feel safe. Mary holds him/ourselves in a way that grants stability but does not deny the dark options in human reality. That makes the cradling experience in the icon a spiritual tableau: a yes to what is and a redemption through what is. Help is perpetually available as a reliable grace so we can live through the conditions of existence and co-redeem the world. In fact, we live through the predicaments of our lives precisely so that we can share in the redemption of our universe.

Our challenge is to bring the gospel of co-creation and co-redemption to life in our lifetime. To say that Mary is our advocate is to acknowledge with joy that we are not alone in this enterprise. A powerful deity in us works with and through us to co-create and co-redeem with us. Soon enough we realize that it is all a gift and that we were meant to be all gratitude, our way of acknowledging the divine origin of our talents. That gratitude leads to humility and egoless love. At the same time, gratitude for our gifts is also a way of feeling comfortable with our own power. This leads to finding our life purpose, which happens when gratitude for our gifts takes the form of giving

them to the world. Notice the beautiful chain of love: from God in me to me and then to all of us.

St. Thomas Aquinas, quoting an earlier source, said, "Goodness is ever diffusive of itself." Our calling is goodness and our goodness automatically spreads itself around. Goodness—Godness—goes on giving. This is why God is not only an inner reality but an outward love and why love of our neighbor is the same as loving God. "Your neighbors are the channel through which all your virtues come to birth," said the mystic St. Catherine of Siena. Here is another striking example of the synchronicity of the Incarnation: Mary brings forth Jesus and the work of God happens on earth as it is in heaven. When we honor Mary as our mother, we ask her to bring us forth. This is the evolutionary plea to let us become co-Christs, co-redeemers.

The feminine images in the Litany of Loreto are consoling and animating. They are ultimately not tools for work but ways of opening to grace. Something, we know not what, is always and everywhere at work, we know not how, but we do know why: so we can release the abundant possibilities of love, wisdom, and healing that are in us and for which the world is waiting.

> *I found in the writings of those great medieval mystics, for whom self-surrender had been the way to self-realization ... that they had found the strength to say Yes to every demand which the needs of their neighbors had made them face, and to say Yes also to every fate life had in store for them.... They found an unreserved acceptance of life, whatever it brought them personally of toil, suffering, or happiness.*   —DAG HAMMARSKJÖLD

Prayer

Mary, thank you for providing an ever-present help to all of us.

Your title Help of Christians began in war, and now we can change it to Help of Humanity by our dedication to end war. Help us in that task.

Place us in the unconditional light as we join you in redeeming a world still lost in the darkness of retaliation and war.

Help us love the world as it is and as it can be.

Let us be held by the timeless while holding the timely.

Hold us by the hand as we engage passionately in the redemption of the world.

Hold us in your arms as we look into the face of danger and evil.

Make us the heroes and heroines who find ways to co-create a world of harmony.

Be Our Lady of victory over war and ego division.

Be our support in bringing help to all those who need us no matter how different, unappealing, or distant.

Be our loving guide in ending divisions among religions.

May we gather together under your mantle of compassion with only one prayer: that we may be one in love.

Mary, join me in commandeering to your love all those still standing at the gate, afraid to come in.

The Titles and the Prayer of Imagination

Prayer is a combination of personal contact with God, the Source, and receiving graces, resources, with gratitude. Most of us have granted precedence to the metaphor of conversation in our description and experience of prayer. We imagine Someone is up above waiting to hear from us, and then he too will speak in some way. We can perhaps find new metaphors for prayer that reflect our unique gifts and excitements. For instance, we can use the metaphor of swimming in the surging ocean of consciousness or of floating in mid-air with no support but that of Spirit.

The limitation of prayer to the conversation model perhaps explains the phrase "the silence of God." Teilhard de Chardin wrote: "A presence is never dumb." Silence is a corollary of the constricting dualistic view of prayer. Once prayer is appreciated as contact with our deepest interior reality, then our own imagination, intuitions, dreams, synchronicities, and awakenings are the voices of God. Nature with all its manifold beauties, the feedback of other humans, and the givens of daily existence are voices too. There is no silence of God, only deafness to God. As Shakespeare says in *The Merchant of Venice:* "There's not the smallest orb which thou beholdst but in his nature like an angel sings. . . . Such harmony is in immortal souls, but whilst this muddy vesture of decay doth grossly close it in, we cannot hear it."

Prayer is any moment of real presence, a personal contact with the divine within, in nature, in the sacraments, in the community, or anywhere where ego is not intrusive. Prayer is a participatory consciousness, not dualistic in any way. Our prayer life is words to music, not words to an audience. Our prayer life is images without words, or silence without images. Images are not only visual but auditory, tactile, olfactory. In short, when St. Paul says: "Pray always," he is describing what we are already and always doing. The challenge is to make it conscious and loving.

We have many ways of knowing. Two such ways are conceptual and perceptual. Plato's ideal was *episteme,* an abstract knowledge that uses concepts arising from the intellect. Aristotle suggested we know more penetratingly through *phronesis,* a practical knowledge that relies on immediate perceptions. This is founded in here and now experience. It arises from the existential moment, from our relationship and response to what is happening. Phronesis/perception is a useful way of understanding how prayer occurs. It is a felt sense and an imaginative response to that which is. "What is" may also be called the will of God, our unfolding destiny of wholeness beckoning to us in each circumstance of our life.

Use the suggestions that follow as points of departure that may foster what is meaningful to you as prayer. These prayer practices expand our vision of prayer so that it is more than words in conversation. Design a contact or form of address that fits your life, beliefs, and gifts. Find ways to turn each prayer into a practice in the world. We can pray by affirmation, writing, art, movement, dance, music, action, silence, responsiveness to nature, intimate love, interpersonal sharing, peeling garlic.

Imagination is an organ of prayer because it arises from the God depths within us and because it accesses so many images of the archetypes. Here are some spiritual and imaginative practices that help us enter more fully into the litany, a treasury of images:

- Work with each image directly. "Compose" comes from Latin words meaning to place together. In art, composition is crucial to the experience of beauty. We respond to words and their inherent images by composing them with our life experiences and by composing our own words around them, like bees around a rose. For instance, if we are facing a question and require discernment, we may pray to Our Lady as Seat of Wisdom while also picturing her on a throne in our hearts and inspiring us with her wisdom about what is happening in our lives.

- Imagine a picture that arises from a title in the litany.

- Explore your own psychological inner feeling space, e.g., your past, your memories of Mary's place in your life and how she can assist you now as she has before.

- Find the symbolic level by engaging a mythic, cosmic sense of continuity with all our ancestors of faith who have prayed to Mary under this title.

- Notice a shift as the doors of perception open to a direct experiential vision without the need for images. Intuition and mysticism begin here.

Images affect and are affected by physical reactions. Images generate similar internal responses as the actual stimuli. Images are the bridges between the conscious processing of information and physical changes, influencing both the voluntary and involuntary nervous system. For example, imagine the morning star or imagine a destructive storm and notice the resultant tranquillity or panic.

An image includes not only a picture but the way we experience it, *a felt sense*. What is the felt sense in you that is stirred by the title you have been moved by? All those who felt this way and feel this way and pray this way are with you in the communion of saints.

Notice new titles for Mary that arise in your consciousness. They are most likely based on what you need as graces and resources for your concerns in the here and now. Images come to you like stars rising in the night sky. When you begin to see your images as visiting realities, not as things you think up, they become your inspiration and may even point to your calling.

Every human predicament has an archetypal symbolic image behind it, e.g., anxiety as a dragon and St. George as its conqueror. Such archetypes hail from the mythic depths of the psyche of humankind, the Source and abode of God.

Work with present feelings so that they may lead you to an image. An image from the litany becomes complete when it includes the dark side of Mary too. For instance, in a depressed state, we may turn to Mary as Morning Star, but first we have to do what she does in the *Pietà:* hold the wounded body. We stay with our feeling of pain and let it speak to us as an image. We then stay with the image as thankful witnesses of it. We may have to stay in the dark before the morning star appears, as the earth itself does every night. To stay with what is leads to meeting the inner Beloved, the wholeness always within us. Mary is our mother both in our pain and in our consolation. As mistress of the conditions of existence she initiates us through pain and leads us out of it when the time is right. A crisis in life liberates us because it blasts us out of limiting containment and opens new vistas. Easter does not cancel good Friday but follows it. Furthermore, the image of the *Pietà* is a completion of the Madonna and Child image that appears at the beginning of the Jesus story. Mary holds us in both birth and rebirth.

Here is a personal example of working with an image: I was feeling depressed and down one morning recently. I sat quietly and let myself feel the depression and my eyes closed by themselves. I suddenly saw a striking and stark image in my mind's eye. It was a black crow sitting on a bare branch. I know that crows live in extended families and never alone, so this made the image more dramatic and unusual. I stared at the image and realized I was feeling alone, abandoned, on a perch with no nourishment. I let that image speak to me without attempting to force a message from it. It showed me a part of myself I was not in touch with and that was asking for attention. Later that day, I found a quotation I had copied out long-hand from Trungpa Rinpoche and that I had forgotten about: "Realizing that the confusion and the chaos in your mind have no origin, no cessation, and nowhere to dwell is a protection."

Later that week I found a poem by Basho, the Haiku artist,

that I had copied out long-hand a few years back and also had forgotten:

> *On a withered bough*
> *A crow has found a perch*
> *And autumn darkens.*

I turned to the Morning Star after this rich personal event, not in place of it. Now I have a complete prayer: acceptance and release: "Yes" to what is and "Go on" to what can be.

Try writing a poem in response to a title that appeals to you. You may also journal a response that uncovers the felt sense of what appeals to you most about it. What appeals to us is what we are ready to explore. Form a prayerful affirmation to bring the message home to you in practical ways. (Appendix Three may be helpful in poetry writing.)

There is often synchronicity—meaningful coincidence—in finding a particular invocation that speaks to you. It may align with similar images or messages from circumstances, dreams, or even comments from other people. Pay close attention to this since synchronicities often point us to our destiny or to a turn our path is about to take.*

The Litany of Loreto contains sentences and silences. Pay attention to the spaces between the titles. They are the fertile silences that may speak to your condition as eloquently as the words.

---

*For more on synchronicity, see David Richo, *Unexpected Miracles: The Gift of Synchronicity and How to Open It* (New York: Crossroad, 1998).

Epilogue

In Venice one day I was sitting in the church of San Zaccaria looking at a painting of the Madonna and Child by Giovanni Bellini while a priest was leading a small congregation in the Litany of Loreto. I was following the titles, and when the priest came to the final title, I was surprised to hear him add one: "Cap-olavoro della Carità." This means Masterpiece of Love. I was unexpectedly awestruck by those words. I felt a yes-and-surprise arise from depths I never quite imagined were in me. I felt myself settle into the utter rightness of this title. It seemed directed to me personally. Suddenly an event in my soul unconjured by me occurred. I could *feel* the love of Mary for me and my love for her all in one instant. I kept looking at the Bellini and realized he must have felt it too and that it was the inspiration of the lu-minous masterpiece he had painted. A lightning bolt of wisdom struck me. I realized that Mary wanted to paint me to look like her Son and that I was meant to be her masterpiece. I knew this was her intention for all of us. Then my heart opened in a new way and I felt a clearer kinship to mother nature and understood in an instant that this universe is *her* masterpiece, meant to be protected and honored like the painting above my head. I under-stood with a certainty never experienced before that nature and the divine and the human are indeed all one. I also knew that Mary is not an invention of the church but the masterpiece of God. I cannot help but gaze at her with wonder and I know my wonder will never be quite expansive enough to appreciate the miracle of such a gift. Imagine being given a mother like this one, I thought. How loved we must be. Then love must be *our* masterpiece. Then love must be.

> *I have loved you with an everlasting love, so I am constant in my affection for you. I have built you once more. You shall be rebuilt, virgin of Israel. Adorned once more and with your tambourines, you will go out dancing gaily.*

> —Jeremiah 31:3–4

Litany Titles

The Litany of Loreto

God our Father in Heaven
God the Son, Redeemer of the world
God the Holy Spirit
Holy Trinity, one God have mercy on us
Holy Mary
Holy Mother of God
Most honored of virgins
Mother of Christ
Mother of the church
Mother of divine grace
Mother most pure
Mother of chaste love
Mother inviolate and undefiled
Mother most amiable
Mother most admirable
Mother of good counsel
Mother of our Creator
Mother of our Savior
Virgin most wise
Virgin rightly praised
Virgin rightly renowned
Virgin most powerful
Virgin gentle in mercy
Faithful virgin

Mirror of justice
Throne of wisdom
Cause of our joy
Vessel of Spirit
Vessel of honor
Vessel of selfless devotion
Mystical Rose
Tower of David
Tower of ivory
House of gold
Ark of the covenant
Gate of heaven
Morning star
Health of the sick
Refuge of sinners
Comfort of the troubled
Help of humanity
Queen of angels
Queen of patriarchs and prophets
Queen of apostles and martyrs
Queen of confessors and virgins
Queen of all saints
Queen conceived without sin
Queen assumed into heaven
Queen of the rosary
Queen of peace: pray for us.
Blessed be the name of the Virgin Mary
now and forever

Gaelic Litany (eighth century)

O great Mary
O Mary, greatest of Marys
O greatest of women
O Queen of angels
O mistress of the heavens

O woman full of the Holy Spirit
O blessed and most blessed
O mother of eternal glory
O mother of the heavenly and earthly church
O mother of love and forgiveness
O mother of the golden heights
O honor of the sky
O sign of serenity
O gate of heaven
O tranquil as the moon
O resplendent as the sun
O canceller of Eve's disgrace
O regeneration of life
O beauty of womanhood
O leader of virgins
O garden enclosed
O closely-locked fountain
O mother of God
O perpetual virgin
O holy virgin
O prudent virgin
O serene virgin
O temple of the living God
O royal throne of the eternal king
O golden casket
O couch of love and mercy
O temple of the divine
O beauty of virgins
O mistress of our tribes
O fountain for the patterned gardens
O cleansing of sin
O purification of souls
O mother of orphans
O solace of the wretched
O star of the sea
O handmaid of the Lord

O mother of Christ
O resort of the Lord
O graceful as the dove
O sanctuary of the Holy Spirit
O virgin of the root of Jesse
O cedar of Mount Lebanon
O cypress of Mount Sion
O crimson rose of the land of Jacob
O blooming like the palm
O fruitful like the olive trees
O glorious son-bearer
O light of Nazareth
O glory of Jerusalem
O beauty of the world
O noblest-born of Christendom
O queen of life
O ladder of heaven:
Pray for us.

Hear the petitions of the poor.
Do not turn away from the wounds and groans of those
    in misery.
Dissolve our trespasses; raise the fallen, feeble, and fettered;
set free the condemned; repair us.
Bestow on us the blossoms and good deeds of virtuous
    living.

Litany of Mary of Nazareth

Glory to you, God our Creator ...
Breathe into us new life, new meaning.
Glory to you, God our Savior ...
Lead us in the way of peace and justice.
Glory to you, healing Spirit ...
Transform us to empower others.
Mary, wellspring of peace ...

Be our guide.
Model of strength
Model of gentleness
Model of trust
Model of courage
Model of patience
Model of risk
Model of openness
Model of perseverance
Mother of the liberator...
Pray for us.
Mother of the homeless
Mother of the dying
Mother of the nonviolent
Mother of widowed mothers
Mother of unwed mothers
Mother of a political prisoner
Mother of the condemned
Mother of the executed criminal
Oppressed woman...
Lead us to life.
Liberator of the oppressed
Marginalized woman
Comforter of the afflicted
Cause of our joy
Sign of contradiction
Breaker of bondage
Political refugee
Seeker of sanctuary
First disciple
Sharer in Christ's passion
Seeker of God's will
Witness to Christ's resurrection
Woman of mercy
Empower us.
Woman of faith

Woman of contemplation
Woman of vision
Woman of wisdom and understanding
Woman of grace and truth
Woman, pregnant with hope
Woman, centered in God
Pray for us.

Mary, Queen of Peace, we entrust our lives to you. Shelter us from war, hatred, and oppression. Teach us to live in peace, to educate ourselves for peace. Inspire us to act justly, to revere all God has made. Root peace firmly in our hearts and in our world. Amen.—*Pax Christi*

Litany of the Sacred Heart
(author's revision)

Heart of Jesus, in whom there is only yes, alive in me for
the good of all humankind
Heart of Jesus, through the heart of Mary, alive in me for
the good of all humankind
Heart of Jesus, center of my heart, alive in me for the good
of all humankind
Heart of Jesus, gate of Paradise, alive in me for the good
of all humankind
Heart of Jesus, aglow with divine love, alive in me for the
good of all humankind
Heart of Jesus, worthy of unending honor, alive in me for
the good of all humankind
Heart of Jesus, replete with all the treasures of wisdom and
knowledge, alive in me for the good of all humankind
Heart of Jesus, from whose fullness we are all receiving,
alive in me for the good of all humankind
Heart of Jesus, desire of the everlasting hills, alive in me
for the good of all humankind

Heart of Jesus, life force of nature and the universe, alive
in me for the good of all humankind

Heart of Jesus, patient and most merciful, alive in me for
the good of all humankind

Heart of Jesus, bountiful to all who turn to you, alive in
me for the good of all humankind

Heart of Jesus, fountain of grace and holiness, alive in me
for the good of all humankind

Heart of Jesus, loving intent behind every twist of fate,
alive in me for the good of all humankind

Heart of Jesus, pierced to open, never to close, alive in me
for the good of all humankind

Heart of Jesus, source of all consolation, alive in me for
the good of all humankind

Heart of Jesus, my life, my death, and my resurrection,
alive in me for the good of all humankind

Heart of Jesus, pledge of eternal tenderness, alive in me
for the good of all humankind

Heart of Jesus, center and joy of nature, alive in me for
the good of all humankind

Heart of Jesus, harmony of all universes, alive in me for
the good of all humankind

Heart of Jesus, consumed with compassion, alive in me for
the good of all humankind

Heart of Jesus, freedom from fear and grasping, alive in
me for the good of all humankind

Heart of Jesus, freedom for generosity and healing, alive
in me for the good of all humankind

Heart of Jesus, design and destiny of every earthly love,
live in me for the evolution of all people and things.

Litany of the Holy Name of Jesus

Jesus, graciously hear us.
God, the Father of heaven
God the Son, Redeemer of the world

God, the Holy Spirit
Holy Trinity, one God
Jesus, Son of the living God
Jesus, splendor of the Father
Jesus, brightness of eternal light
Jesus, king of glory
Jesus, the sun of justice
Jesus, son of the Virgin Mary
Jesus, amiable and admirable
Jesus, powerful God
Jesus, father of the world to come
Jesus, angel of the great council
Jesus, most powerful
Jesus, most patient, obedient, meek, and humble of heart
Jesus, lover of chastity
Jesus, lover of us
Jesus, God of peace
Jesus, author of life
Jesus, model of all virtues
Jesus, zealous for souls
Jesus, our God and our refuge
Jesus, father of the poor
Jesus, treasure of the faithful
Jesus, good shepherd
Jesus, true light, eternal wisdom, and infinite goodness
Jesus, our way and our life
Jesus, joy of angels
Jesus, king of patriarchs
Jesus, master of apostles
Jesus, teacher of the evangelists
Jesus, strength of martyrs
Jesus, light of confessors
Jesus, purity of virgins
Jesus, crown of all saints
Be merciful and graciously hear us, O Jesus.

Appendix Two

The Shadow

The shadow is comprised of our negative traits and our positive powers.* The negative shadow is the dark side of the ego. The positive shadow is its bright potential. The shadow refers to our reactions to the characteristics of others' personality, not to their actions or behavior. The shadow affects us wherever, whenever, and in whomever we encounter it. It is not limited to any one occasion or person. If a negative quality in only one person upsets us or we are personally insulted by just one person, it may be simply an affront to our ego, not a projection of our shadow. Likewise, if a trait or quality in someone else *informs* us about his personality but does not *affect* us, it is not the shadow.

The shadow becomes out of control and regressive only when it is repressed. In popular lore, the devil (the archetypal negative shadow) is ugly: cloven hoofs, horns, tail, etc. Such a description is based on this principle. The shadow indeed looks terrifying when it remains unintegrated. The work is to tame and redirect its energy. Jung says: "Any part of myself that I do not accept unconditionally splits off and becomes more and more primitive." St. Catherine of Siena speaking of Satan adds: "Don't be afraid of the old pickpocket."

Our unconscious repressed shadow arises into consciousness through projection. The best way the shadow can be found out

---

*See David Richo, *Shadow Dance: Liberating the Power and Creativity of Your Dark Side* (Boston: Shambhala, 1999) for a fuller view and for practices that help you integrate the shadow. That book also explores the question of the shadow of God.

is through a strong reaction to someone else: repulsion by something unwholesome or attraction to or idealization of something
appealing. The other person usually has the quality we are re-
acting to, but the intensity of our reaction tells us more is going
on: we are meeting up with an ordinarily denied part of ourselves. We are *projecting* our own repressed and fragmented
self. Both positive and negative reactions to others call upon
us to do the work of personal integration. The task is to with-
draw the projections and thereby reclaim our lost or doubted
horizons.

To hate the serial murders of Ted Bundy does not mean that
we are serial killers. To admire the tennis proficiency of a pro
does not mean that we are pros too. The shadow side of us is
revealed in our strong projective responses to the qualities from
which actions flow. The actions themselves evoke reactions but
are not to be taken literally as reflective of the same inclinations
in us. Psychopathic behavior flows from mental illness. Acumen
in sports happens because of natural skill and persevering practice. Our strong reactions are simply appropriate to the extreme
badness or skillfulness of what we see.

The negative shadow lies hidden because of the fear of loss
of approval or of empathic responsiveness by others who see
it. In fact, the shadow is anything about us that has not been
mirrored, not looked into with loving acceptance. The positive
shadow is kept hidden because we believe it is too powerful for
us or anyone to see. We doubt our own depths and the extent of
our powers and virtues. Many early growth-negating messages
may account for this self-diminishing. The sad result of it all is
that we store in the cellar or attic what could be useful in our
psychic house!

The shadow is personal when it is about ourselves and others.
It is collective when it is about humanity and its penchant to produce miraculous goodness that expands us or nefarious evil that
destroys us. Specific people come along in positive and negative
collective shadow categories and are idolized or demonized as
a result. Both these saints and sinners are often feverishly fol-

lowed by individuals who are thereby caught up in something larger than themselves.

The shadow is as vast as the unconscious and can never be totally known or integrated. This is because it is continually and creatively forming new configurations throughout life. (It is like our memory bank. Memories are a selection, not a collection, of images about our past. We select them anew at each phase of our lives and thus they are continually revised.) Our practice of befriending our shadow is humbling since we soon discover it will take a whole lifetime to deal with only the tip of its iceberg. To befriend the shadow is to work with whatever of it may reveal itself to us moment by moment. If we are sincere in our enterprise, willing to see what is see-able and do what is do-able, we can trust that even a little progress is healthy adequate integration.

The personal shadow is befriended by us as individuals. The collective shadow requires a mass response; no one person can really handle it all. St. George, Hercules, and other heroes of myth are projections of our ego's wish that we could. According to Elie Wiesel, "There is no messiah but there are messianic moments in which *we* humanize destiny." This does not mean being superhuman but being fully realized as human.

Befriending the shadow means that we face and then transform what is unacceptable in ourselves. We thereby uncover the good that is untapped in ourselves. Our unredeemed worst is our untapped best! The negative shadow and the positive shadow are thus ultimately revealed as one and the same coin with two sides, both contributing to its value. "Dark is what brings out your light," writes Robert Frost. Leviathan and Behemoth are carved and consumed, not chucked (1 Enoch 60:10).

The practice of befriending is based on our effort but also requires the completing action of grace, a power beyond our ego. We take the steps and then, often, shifts happen inside us that reveal and give us access to more riches than we may ever have expected in ourselves. For instance, as we befriend our shadow trait of being controlling of others, a shift occurs and we let go of that style. Then we notice our children and friends are listening to us with more respect. Synchronous events may follow and we are given some leadership opportunities. We ventured the risky steps to free ourselves of our controlling ways and then, as a natural consequence, our untapped potential for leadership opened. This is how we act in accord with our destiny and make a contribution to the world through our shadow work and its assisting graces.

The shadow is the opposite of the visible persona. This does not mean that someone with great love also equally hates others. What is visible in external action rather shows the *capacity* for the alternative. Those who love have an equal capacity for hate; those who hate have an equal capacity for love.

Dorothy successfully confronted the witch when she first arrived in Oz by taking possession of the ruby slippers. It was out of character for her to take something that was not hers. Going out of character is a clue to the fact that something spiritual is afoot. The heroic initiate is faced with demands to find unusual supports (the scarecrow, tin man, and cowardly lion), new behaviors (talking to trees, destroying the witch). The struggle gains depth when the heroine sees that she is herself the witch and the heroine. To overcome the shadow is not to kill it off but to become conscious of this identical darker side in oneself. Dorothy probably learned that one later day in her life when she noticed herself scolding a little neighbor girl about her pesky dog.

One does not become conscious by imagining figures of light but by making the darkness conscious.

— CARL JUNG

Poetry Making

Apollo was venerated in ancient Greece as the god of light and healing as well as poetry. It seems that poetry was therefore associated with healing and light from earliest times. Mary is the poet of the Magnificat. A poem confronts us with an immediate feeling through the medium of images that can evoke healing power. Within each of us is the poet-guide archetype who transfigures images. We contact this assisting force in our psyche when we write a poem or respond to one.

Wallace Stevens spoke of "the essential poem at the heart of things." Poetry is the soul's language, and everyone is capable of speaking it. It has the power to render immediate feelings in the compelling rhythms of the imagination. When we write a poem, we locate personal metaphors that escort us to the unopened rooms in our psyche. We discover some images that have lain dormant in us for decades and some that are lively at this moment. We work with images that visualize, not with words that conceptualize, in order to access the full spectrum of our inner colors. We fashion them into a poetic diction that is faithful to our unique needs and visions. Every poem is indeed an example of what Jung called "active imagination," extending unconscious realities into conscious images. In active imagination the implicit becomes explicit. To move from the unconscious to consciousness is another example of the Resurrection archetype at work. We suddenly awake to see how our story, and especially its present chapter, fit into a vaster volume of our destiny.

Poetry differs from prose in that it is fresh, concrete, arresting, and economical. Poetry makes a *Thou* of experience: a reality that comes from outside but is incomplete until it finds a personal resonance in us. The rhythms of poetry are commanding because they remind us that we are composed of rhythms: our life is measured in chords and intervals. When we write a poem we simultaneously evoke the power that we express in poetic form.

The creative process is the unconscious activation of archetypal images and elaboration of these images into a finished work. Poems we write today bring up answers to questions we may pose only later, since in the unconscious there is no linear time. Images stay with us because they still have something to say. Poetry is how we say it. Poems often expose what has been overlooked. Poetry thus gently beguiles us into a deeper part of ourselves. The rational mind offers insufficient tools in the quest for self-knowledge. In poetry our tools are more adventuresome and expansive. We have imagistic intuitive discernment, knowledge beyond words. That takes precedence over left-brain thinking, knowledge that can be put into words. The poetic imagination is thus the missing link to the fullness of our human, spiritual reality.

Here is a disturbing passage from the journal of Charles Darwin:

> I have also said that formerly pictures and also music gave me great delight. But now, for many years, I cannot endure to react to a line of poetry. I have tried lately to read Shakespeare and found it so intolerably dull that it nauseated me. I have also lost my taste for pictures and music. . . . My mind seems to have been grinding loaves out of large collections of facts, but why this should have caused the atrophy of that part of the brain, on which the higher states depend, I cannot conceive. A man with a mind more highly organized or better constituted than mine would not, I suppose, thus have suffered: and if I had to live my life again, I would have made it a rule to read some poetry and listen to some

music at least once a week: for perhaps the part of my brain now atrophied would have thus kept active through use.

The body is the densest part of the unconscious, so body resonance is crucial if a poem is to happen. Tune into a felt sense of the image that has emerged for you in a quotation. Feel your body resonate to it. Gather words that declare what you feel. Use all five senses. Employ metaphors and similes wherever you can. Do not rhyme. Listen and let reality give you building blocks. Then take this channeled information and construct it in an economical way. You can produce a feeling-laden impact through a pictured representation. It is important not to engage in interpretation, abstraction, or moralizing—good advice for life in general.

Works Consulted

Biskupek, A. *Our Lady's Litany: Readings and Reflections*. Milwaukee: Bruce Publications, 1954.

Blunt, Hugh. *Listen, Mother of God*. Ozone Park, N.Y.: Catholic Literary Guild, 1940.

Bonnet, Leon. *Our Lady Speaks*. Trans. Leonard J. Doyle. St. Meinrad, Ind.: Grail Publications, 1954.

Brown, Raymond. *The Birth of the Messiah: A Commentary on the Infancy Narratives in the Gospels of Matthew and Luke*. New York: Doubleday, 1993.

Cantalamessa, Raniero. *Mary, Mirror of the Church*. Collegeville, Minn.: Liturgical Press, 1992.

Cassidy, James. *The Old Irish Love of the Blessed Virgin Mary*. Dublin: Gill and Son, 1933.

Christ, Carol, and Judith Plaskow. *Womanspirit Rising: A Feminist Reader in Religion*. San Francisco: Harper & Row, 1979.

Craighead, Meinrad: *The Mothers's Songs: Images of God and the Mother*. Mahwah, N.J.: Paulist, 1986.

Crichton, J. D. *Our Lady in the Liturgy*. Collegeville, Minn.: Liturgical Press, 1997.

Crossan, John Dominic. *The Birth of Christianity: Discovering What Happened in the Years Immediately after the Execution of Jesus*. San Francisco: HarperSanFrancisco, 1998.

Daly, Mary. *Beyond God the Father*. Boston: Beacon, 1973.

Dollen, Charles. *Listen, Mother of God: Reflections on the Litany of Loreto*. Huntington, Ind.: Our Sunday Visitor, 1989.

Edinger, Edward. *The Eternal Drama: The Inner Meaning of Greek Mythology*. Boston: Shambhala, 1994.

———. *The Mysterium Lectures: A Journey through C. G. Jung's Mysterium Coniunctionis*. Toronto: Inner City, 1995.

Eisler, Riane. *The Chalice and the Blade: Our History, Our Future.* San Francisco: Harper & Row, 1988.

———. *Sacred Pleasure: Sex, Myth, and the Politics of the Body.* San Francisco: HarperSanFrancisco, 1995.

Galland, China. *Longing for Darkness: Tara and the Black Madonna.* New York: Penguin, 1990.

Gillet, Louis. *Immaculata: Thoughts on Mary's Litany.* West Chester, Pa.: Villa Maria, 1945.

Gimbutas, Marija. *The Language of the Goddess.* San Francisco: Harper, 1989.

Hahn, Scott. *Hail, Holy Queen: The Mother of God in the Word of God.* New York: Doubleday, 2001.

Harding, Esther. *Woman's Mysteries.* New York: Putnam, 1971.

James, Edwin. *The Cult of the Mother Goddess.* London: Thames and Hudson, 1959.

Johnson, Elizabeth. *Consider Jesus: Waves of Renewal in Christology.* New York: Crossroad, 1992.

———. *She Who Is: The Mystery of God in a Feminist Theological Perspective.* New York: Crossroad, 1992.

Jung, Carl. *Psychology and Alchemy.* Princeton, N.J.: Princeton University Press, 1953.

———. Jung, Carl. *The Archetypes and the Collective Unconscious.* Princeton, N.J.: Princeton University Press, 1953.

Layard, John. *The Virgin Archetype.* Zurich: Spring, 1972.

Le Buffe, Francis, S.J. *Litany of Our Lady.* New York: America Press, 1931.

Mato, Tataya. *The Black Madonna Within: Drawings, Dreams, and Reflections.* Chicago: Open Court, 1994.

Motz, Lotte. *Faces of the Goddess.* New York: Oxford University Press, 1997.

Neumann, Erich. *The Great Mother: An Analysis of the Archetype.* Trans. Ralph Manheim. Princeton, N.J.: Princeton University Press, 1955.

O'Connell, C. G. *The Life of the Blessed Virgin Mary as Set Forth in Her Litany.* Baltimore: Murphy Publishing, 1914.

Pagels, Elaine. *Adam, Eve, and the Serpent.* New York: Random House, 1989.

Patai, Raphael. *The Hebrew Goddess.* New York: Avon, 1978.

Rahner, Hugo. *Greek Myths and Christian Mystery.* New York: Harper & Row, 1963.

Ranke-Heinemann, Uta. *Eunuchs for the Kingdom of Heaven.* New York: Doubleday, 1990.

Ruddick, Sara. *Maternal Thinking: Toward a Politics of Peace.* New York: Ballantine, 1989.

Schaberg, Jane. *The Illegitimacy of Jesus: A Feminist Theological Interpretation of the Infancy Narratives.* New York: Crossroad, 1990.

Smart, Ninian. *The Religious Experience of Mankind.* New York: Scribner, 1976.

Smith, Huston. *The World's Religions: Our Great Wisdom Traditions.* San Francisco: HarperSanFrancisco, 1991.

Spretnak, C. *The Politics of Women's Spirituality.* Garden City. N.Y.: Anchor Books, 1982.

Ward, Benedicta. *Harlots of the Desert: A Study of Repentance in Early Monastic Sources.* Kalamazoo, Mich.: Cistercian Publications, 1987.

Warner, Marina. *Alone of All Her Sex: The Myth and the Cult of the Virgin Mary.* New York: Knopf, 1976.

About the Author

David Richo, Ph.D., M.F.T., is a psychotherapist, teacher, and writer
in Santa Barbara and in San Francisco, who emphasizes Jungian,
transpersonal, and spiritual perspectives in his work.
He teaches at Santa Barbara City College Adult Education,
University of California at Berkeley Extension, and at Esalen.

He is the author of

How to Be an Adult
(Paulist, 1991)

When Love Meets Fear
(Paulist, 1997)

Unexpected Miracles:
The Gift of Synchronicity and How to Open It
(Crossroad, 1998)

Shadow Dance:
Liberating the Power and Creativity of Your Dark Side
(Shambhala, 1999)

Catholic Means Universal:
Integrating Spirituality and Religion
(Crossroad, 2000)

Richo gives workshops across the country, some of which are audiotaped.
For a catalog send a self-addressed, single-stamped, legal-size envelope to:

DR, Box 31027, Santa Barbara, CA 93130.

On the web at: davericho.com